Life After Death

True Near-Death Experiences to Give Emotional Comfort and Spiritual Inspiration

Molly Hooper

Table of Contents

Introduction	3
Ian McCormack: Jellyfish Sting	8
Anita Moorjani: Embracing Unconditional Love	13
Dr. Eben Alexander: Proof of Heaven	18
Howard Storm: From Darkness to Light	23
Pam Reynolds: Seeing Beyond Death	28
Don Piper: Ninety Minutes in Eternity	33
Colton Burpo: A Child's Journey to Heaven	38
Vicki Noratuk: The Blind Woman Who "Saw" During Her NDE	43
Dr. Mary Neal: Between Two Worlds	47
Mellen-Thomas Benedict : Journey Through the Light and Back	51
George Ritchie: The Christmas Eve Journey	56
Betty Eadie: Embraced by the Light	61
Nancy Rynes: Messages from the Divine	66
Colleen Smith: A Leap of Faith	71
Thomas Welch: A Doctor's Revelation	76
Brian Miller: The Spirit Guides	82
Al Sullivan: A Shared Journey Beyond	87
Janet Tarantino: Three Strikes and You're In	92
Jim McCartney: The Sound of Music Beyond the Veil	97
Dr. Rajiv Parti: A Journey Through Karma and Compassion	102
Stephanie Arnold: Premonitions, Death, and the Power of Intuition	107
Tricia Barker: Angels in the OR	112
Jeff Olsen: Love Beyond the Veil	117
Ellyn Dye: A Kaleidoscope of Creation	122
Conclusion	127

© Copyright Molly Hooper 2024 - All rights reserved.

The content within this book may not be reproduced, duplicated or transmitted without direct written permission from the author or the publisher.

Under no circumstances will any blame or legal responsibility be held against the publisher, or author, for any damages, reparation, or monetary loss due to the information contained within this book. Either directly or indirectly. You are responsible for your own choices, actions, and results.

Legal Notice:

This book is copyright protected. This book is only for personal use. You cannot amend, distribute, sell, use, quote or paraphrase any part, of the content within this book, without the consent of the author or publisher.

Disclaimer Notice:

Please note the information contained within this document is for educational and entertainment purposes only. All effort has been expended to present accurate, up-to-date, and reliable, complete information. No warranties of any kind are declared or implied. Readers acknowledge that the author is not engaging in the rendering of legal, financial, medical or professional advice. The content within this book has been derived from various sources. Please consult a licensed professional before attempting any techniques outlined in this book.

By reading this document, the reader agrees that under no circumstances is the author responsible for any losses, direct or indirect, which are incurred as a result of the use of the information contained within this document, including, but not limited to, — errors, omissions, or inaccuracies.

Introduction

> "You don't have a soul. You are a soul. You have a body."
> C.S. Lewis

What lies beyond the veil of death? It's a question that has haunted humanity since the dawn of time, a mystery that transcends culture, religion, and science. For centuries, we've sought answers through philosophy, spirituality, and scientific exploration, yearning to understand what awaits us on the other side. Are we met with darkness, or is there light? Is there a continuation of consciousness, or do we simply cease to be? These are the questions that near-death experiences (NDEs) attempt to answer, offering glimpses into a world that remains tantalizingly out of reach.

This book brings together some of the most compelling accounts of NDEs, each a deeply personal journey into realms of love, light, and infinite possibility. From vibrant kaleidoscopes of color to encounters with spiritual beings, from life reviews that reveal the interconnectedness of all things to cosmic insights that challenge our understanding of reality, these stories paint a picture of existence far greater and more profound than we can imagine. They are not just tales of the afterlife—they are reminders of the beauty, purpose, and interconnectedness of life itself.

The accounts shared in these pages come from people of all walks of life: scientists and skeptics, artists and teachers, parents and children. Despite their diverse backgrounds, they share one commonality: each individual faced death and returned with an extraordinary story to tell. Their experiences challenge conventional notions of reality, inviting us to reconsider what it means to live, to die, and to love.

One of the most fascinating aspects of NDEs is their universality. Across cultures and belief systems, people report remarkably similar experiences. Many describe being enveloped by a radiant light that exudes unconditional love and peace. Others recount traveling through tunnels, encountering deceased loved ones, or visiting realms of indescribable beauty. Some undergo life reviews, where they see the impact of their actions on others, often with profound emotional clarity. These recurring themes suggest that NDEs are not just isolated events but part of a larger, universal phenomenon.

The stories in this book are not bound by religious or cultural frameworks. While some individuals interpret their experiences through the lens of their faith, others find their worldviews expanded in ways that defy traditional beliefs. This diversity of interpretation highlights the deeply personal nature of NDEs, as well as their capacity to transcend the boundaries of doctrine and dogma. Regardless of one's beliefs, these stories invite us to explore the possibility of a reality that exists beyond what we can see, touch, or measure.

At their core, NDEs are not just about what happens after death; they are about what it means to live. Those who return from the brink often describe a newfound appreciation for life's simplest joys: the warmth of the sun on their skin, the laughter of a child, the interconnectedness of all living things. They speak of a love so pure and unconditional that it reshapes their relationships and priorities. They emphasize the importance of kindness, compassion, and living with intention.

These experiences also provide profound insights into death itself. For many, the fear of dying diminishes or disappears entirely after an NDE. They describe death not as an end but as a transition, a doorway to a greater reality. This perspective can be deeply comforting, not only for those who have faced death firsthand but also for those grieving the loss of loved ones. NDEs remind us that love endures, that connections persist, and that life is part of an infinite, ongoing journey.

In recent decades, the study of NDEs has gained significant attention from scientists and researchers. Advances in neuroscience and cardiology have allowed for more detailed examinations of the physiological and psychological aspects of these experiences. While some argue that NDEs can be explained as hallucinations caused by a dying brain, others point to the consistency and depth of these accounts as evidence of something beyond the physical.

For example, cases like Pam Reynolds, who described vivid details of her surgery while clinically brain-dead, challenge purely materialistic explanations. Similarly, studies have shown that individuals blind from birth have reported visual experiences during NDEs, raising questions about the nature of perception and consciousness. These stories blur the line between science and spirituality, suggesting that the two may not be as separate as they seem.

While this book does not aim to settle the debate, it embraces the mystery. It invites readers to ponder the possibilities, to approach these stories with curiosity and an open mind. Whether you view NDEs as spiritual revelations, psychological phenomena, or something in between, their transformative power is undeniable.

Each story in this book is a journey of transformation. Dr. Eben Alexander, a neurosurgeon who once dismissed NDEs as fantasies, was forever changed by his own experience of a heavenly realm. Stephanie Arnold's premonitions and subsequent NDE during childbirth strengthened her belief in the power of intuition. Ellyn Dye's kaleidoscopic journey revealed the interconnectedness of all life and the creative energy that fuels the universe.

These transformations extend beyond the individuals who experience them. Their stories ripple outward, touching the lives of family members, friends, and strangers. They inspire hope, spark curiosity, and encourage us to live more fully. They remind us that even in our darkest moments, there is light—and that light is within us all.

In a world often consumed by division, materialism, and fear, NDEs offer a powerful counterpoint. They speak of love as the essence of existence, of our profound connection to one another and to the universe. They challenge us to look beyond our differences and to see the shared humanity that binds us.

They remind us that life is precious, fleeting, and filled with opportunities for growth and connection.

Whether you are a skeptic or a believer, a seeker or a scientist, these stories have the power to move you. They invite you to question, to reflect, and to wonder. What if consciousness does not end with death? What if love truly is the driving force of the universe? What if every moment, every choice, every connection matters more than we realize?

As you read these accounts, I encourage you to approach them with an open heart and mind. Let yourself be drawn into the vivid imagery, the profound insights, and the transformative journeys these individuals have shared. Allow their stories to inspire you, to challenge your assumptions, and to deepen your appreciation for the mystery and wonder of life.

This book is not about providing definitive answers; it's about exploring possibilities. It's about celebrating the courage of those who have faced death and returned with messages of hope and love. It's about reminding us all that, no matter what lies beyond, the journey of life is a gift—a symphony of moments, connections, and experiences that shape who we are.

So, turn the page and step into the light. What you'll find may forever change the way you see the world, yourself, and the infinite possibilities that lie ahead.

Ian McCormack: Jellyfish Sting

Ian McCormack was a young adventurer and surfer who lived for the thrill of the ocean. Born and raised in New Zealand, he had a love for the sea that carried him across the globe in search of the perfect wave. During his travels, Ian explored exotic locales, eventually finding himself on the idyllic island of Mauritius in the Indian Ocean. Unbeknownst to him, a simple evening swim would lead to a life-altering encounter with death—and beyond.

One evening, Ian and his friends decided to go night diving for lobsters. The warm waters off the coast of Mauritius were alive with marine life, and Ian felt at home in the ocean's embrace. As the group dove under the moonlit waves, Ian swam a little farther from the others, lost in the excitement of the hunt. Suddenly, he felt a sharp, burning pain in his arm. Looking down, he realized he had been stung by a box jellyfish, one of the most venomous creatures in the ocean.

At first, Ian dismissed the sting as a minor inconvenience. But within moments, his arm began to swell, and a fiery sensation coursed through his body. Ian had no idea that the venom of the box jellyfish could kill a human within minutes. When he was stung again on the same dive, the situation became dire. Struggling to swim back to the boat, he signaled for help, but his strength was rapidly fading.

Ian's friends managed to get him back to shore, but by then, the venom had spread through his body, causing excruciating pain and paralysis. He was rushed to a local hospital, but the journey was long, and Ian felt his life slipping away with each passing second. His vision blurred, his breathing became labored, and his heart pounded in his chest. He began to feel a strange detachment from his body, as though he were floating outside of himself.

As the ambulance sped through the night, Ian's thoughts turned to his life. He had grown up in a Christian family but had drifted away from faith as a young man. Now, on the brink of death, he found himself overwhelmed with regret and fear. In a desperate plea, he cried out to God: "If you're real, help me. Forgive me for my sins."

By the time Ian arrived at the hospital, he was unconscious. Medical staff tried to revive him, but his body gave out, and he was pronounced clinically dead. It was at this moment that Ian's extraordinary journey began.

He found himself in a realm of utter darkness. At first, Ian was confused, unsure of where he was or what was happening. The darkness was thick, oppressive, and cold, unlike anything he had ever experienced. He felt an overwhelming sense of loneliness and despair, as though he had been cast into a void devoid of life and hope.

Suddenly, Ian became aware of other beings in the darkness. He couldn't see them clearly, but their presence was menacing. They mocked and taunted him, their voices filled with malice. Ian realized he was in a place he could only describe as hell. The experience was terrifying, and he felt an intense longing to escape.

Just as Ian felt he might be lost forever, a radiant light appeared in the distance. The light grew brighter and more inviting, cutting through the darkness like a beacon of hope. Ian felt himself being drawn toward it, as though it were calling him. As he moved closer, the light enveloped him in warmth and love, washing away the fear and pain he had felt moments before.

Ian described the light as unlike anything on Earth—pure, brilliant, and alive. It wasn't just light; it was a presence, one that Ian instinctively knew to be God. In the presence of this divine being, Ian felt an overwhelming sense of peace and unconditional love. He realized that he was being given a second chance, a chance to understand the meaning of life and his place in the universe.

As Ian stood in the light, he saw glimpses of a heavenly realm. It was a place of indescribable beauty, filled with vibrant colors and a sense of perfect harmony. He felt a deep connection to everything around him, as though he were part of something infinitely greater than himself. In this place, Ian encountered a being who he believed to be Jesus. The being radiated compassion and understanding, and Ian felt his soul laid bare before Him.

During this encounter, Ian was shown moments from his life and the choices he had made. He realized the impact of his actions, both good and bad, and felt a profound sense of humility. Yet, despite his mistakes, the love he felt in the presence of the divine was unwavering. He understood that he was forgiven and that his life had a purpose yet to be fulfilled.

At a certain point, Ian was given a choice: to stay in this heavenly realm or to return to his earthly life. Although the idea of remaining in the light was tempting, Ian felt a deep conviction that his time on Earth was not yet over. He knew he needed to share what he had experienced and to live a life aligned with the truths he had learned.

With that decision, Ian found himself back in his body. The pain and paralysis returned, but his spirit was transformed. Against all odds, Ian began to recover. The doctors were astonished, as the venom from the jellyfish sting should have been fatal. Ian believed his recovery was nothing short of a miracle.

The near-death experience left Ian with a renewed sense of purpose and faith. He returned to New Zealand and dedicated his life to sharing his story with others. His experience profoundly impacted everyone who heard it, offering hope and inspiration to those struggling with questions about life, death, and the existence of God.

Ian's story has since been shared in books, interviews, and even a film titled *The Perfect Wave*. His message is simple yet profound: life is a gift, and we are all deeply loved by a higher power. For Ian, his brush with death was not an end, but a beginning—a chance to live with clarity, purpose, and gratitude.

Ian McCormack's near-death experience continues to resonate with people around the world, serving as a powerful testament to the mysteries of life, death, and the human spirit.

Anita Moorjani: Embracing Unconditional Love

Anita Moorjani's story is one of the most profound and inspiring accounts of a near-death experience (NDE). Her remarkable journey, detailed in her book *Dying to Be Me*, has touched millions worldwide, offering hope, healing, and a fresh perspective on life and death.

Anita was a successful woman living in Hong Kong, navigating the complexities of her Indian cultural heritage and Western upbringing. For much of her life, she was plagued by fear—fear of illness, failure, and not meeting societal expectations. This fear manifested in a constant need to please others, a habit that drained her emotionally and physically.

In 2002, Anita was diagnosed with Hodgkin's lymphoma, a form of cancer that ravaged her body over the course of four years. Despite trying various treatments, her condition worsened. By February 2006, her body had become a fragile shell. Her muscles had atrophied, her organs were shutting down, and she was unable to eat or walk. On the morning of February 2, 2006,

Anita slipped into a coma. Her doctors informed her family that she was in the final stages of her illness and would likely not survive the day.

As Anita's body lay lifeless in the hospital bed, she found herself awakening—not in her physical body but in an entirely different realm. She described the experience as feeling "more alive than ever." The world she entered was radiant, filled with unconditional love and a sense of boundless expansion. Time and space ceased to exist in the way she understood them; everything was interconnected, and all answers to life's questions were instantly accessible.

Anita experienced a heightened state of awareness, where she could see and hear events happening both in the hospital and far away. She observed her distraught family at her bedside, including her husband, Danny, pleading with her to come back. At the same time, she became aware of her brother, who was on a plane rushing to see her one last time. Astonishingly, she could even feel the emotions of each person, understanding their thoughts and intentions in ways that transcended ordinary perception.

The most profound aspect of Anita's experience was her encounter with an overwhelming sense of love. She felt enveloped in a divine, unconditional love that removed all fear and pain. In this state, she realized that her true essence was not her physical body but her eternal, infinite soul. She described this as a "state of pure consciousness," where she was one with the universe yet still uniquely herself.

Anita encountered what she interpreted as the essence of her father, who had passed away years earlier. His presence was comforting, familiar, and filled with understanding. He communicated to her—not in words but through a shared knowing—that it was not her time to die. Yet, Anita felt no pressure to return; she was given a choice to either come back to her physical life or remain in this blissful state.

In this realm, Anita gained profound insights into the nature of life, health, and the human condition. She understood that her cancer was not an external enemy but a manifestation of the fears and self-doubt she had harbored for years. Her desire to please others and suppress her own needs had created a toxic environment within her body, eventually leading to her illness.

She also realized that the universe operates on love and connection. She saw that every individual is a vital part of the whole, each carrying unique gifts and a purpose. The judgments, fears, and limitations we place on ourselves are illusions that hinder us from living authentically.

Perhaps the most striking realization was that she was inherently worthy of love, simply by existing. Anita described this as understanding her "magnificence" for the first time. She saw that every being, regardless of their actions or status, is a reflection of the divine.

Though the otherworldly realm offered her peace and freedom, Anita became aware of the impact her death would have on her loved ones. She also understood that her journey was not yet complete; she had more to experience and share with the world. With this newfound awareness, she made the decision to return to her body.

Before she returned, Anita received a clear message: her body would heal if she chose to go back. The knowledge she had gained in this realm would guide her to a life free from fear and illness. This promise filled her with confidence as she re-entered her physical form.

To the astonishment of her doctors and family, Anita regained consciousness within hours. She felt an incredible sense of clarity and vitality, even though her body was still frail. Over the next few days, her condition improved at an unprecedented rate. Tumors that had once been the size of lemons began to shrink rapidly, and her organs resumed functioning.

Within weeks, Anita was cancer-free. Doctors conducted multiple tests, unable to explain the sudden disappearance of the disease. The medical community was baffled, yet Anita knew her recovery was tied to the profound truths she had experienced during her NDE.

Anita's near-death experience fundamentally transformed her outlook on life. She no longer lived in fear of illness, failure, or the opinions of others. Instead, she embraced life with joy, authenticity, and gratitude. She began sharing her story to inspire others to reconnect with their own magnificence.

Her message emphasizes the importance of self-love and living authentically. She encourages people to let go of fear and trust in the universe's inherent benevolence. According to Anita, the key to a fulfilling life is recognizing that we are already whole, worthy, and deeply connected to all of existence.

Anita Moorjani's story has resonated with people across the globe. Her book *Dying to Be Me* became a bestseller, and she has since traveled extensively, sharing her message through talks, workshops, and interviews. Her experience has been studied by researchers and cited as a powerful example of the healing potential of consciousness.

In sharing her journey, Anita has helped countless individuals overcome their fears and embrace their lives with renewed purpose. Her NDE is not only a tale of miraculous recovery but also a testament to the transformative power of love, awareness, and self-acceptance.

Anita's story reminds us that life is a precious gift and that healing—whether physical, emotional, or spiritual—is always possible when we align with our true selves. Her near-death experience is a beacon of hope, illustrating that even in the darkest moments, we are surrounded by light and love.

Dr. Eben Alexander: Proof of Heaven

Dr. Eben Alexander was a highly accomplished neurosurgeon with decades of experience. As a man of science, he was skeptical of spiritual phenomena, often dismissing near-death experiences as the brain's way of coping with trauma. However, his skepticism was profoundly challenged in 2008 when he himself had an NDE during a seven-day coma caused by a rare and aggressive bacterial meningitis.

Before the illness struck, Dr. Alexander lived a life deeply rooted in logic and reason. He prided himself on his scientific understanding of the brain and firmly believed that consciousness was a product of the brain's neural networks. To him, stories of heavenly realms and spiritual encounters were nothing more than fantasies or hallucinations. His perspective on the universe was entirely materialistic—until the morning when he woke up with a splitting headache.

What began as a headache quickly escalated into something far more severe. Dr. Alexander became disoriented, feverish, and unable to articulate his thoughts. His family rushed him to the hospital, where doctors discovered he had contracted E. coli meningitis, a rare but devastating bacterial infection that targets the brain's protective membranes. The infection was so severe that his brain's neocortex—the part responsible for higher-order functions like perception and thought—was completely shut down.

Within hours, Dr. Alexander slipped into a deep coma. His prognosis was grim; the likelihood of recovery was virtually nonexistent. His colleagues and family prepared for the worst, believing his brain had suffered irreparable damage.

Dr. Alexander's journey started in darkness. He found himself in what he later described as a murky, primitive state of existence. It was a "void" that felt infinite yet contained a sense of comfort and safety. He had no awareness of his earthly identity—no memory of being a father, husband, or neurosurgeon. He was simply a being of consciousness, detached from the physical world.

In this void, he encountered a curious sound: a deep, rhythmic vibration that seemed to grow louder and more complex. Suddenly, a light appeared, cutting through the darkness and pulling him upward with an irresistible force. The transition was instantaneous and breathtaking.

Dr. Alexander emerged into a realm of indescribable beauty and vibrancy, far beyond anything he had experienced in the physical world. He described this place as a "gateway" to the afterlife—a landscape teeming with colors, textures, and patterns that defied earthly understanding. Everything glowed with a divine brilliance, and the air seemed alive with music that wasn't just heard but felt on a soul-deep level.

In this heavenly realm, he encountered a being of immense love and light. She appeared as a beautiful young woman, radiating warmth and compassion. Although he didn't recognize her, he felt an immediate connection with her, as if she had always been a part of his existence. She communicated with him telepathically, conveying messages of profound significance: " You are loved. You are cherished. You have nothing to fear. "

Dr. Alexander marveled at the overwhelming sense of acceptance and unity he felt. There was no judgment, no anxiety—only a pure, all-encompassing love that seemed to permeate everything around him.

With the guidance of the woman, Dr. Alexander ascended to an even higher dimension, which he called the "Core." This realm was the pinnacle of his journey—a place of infinite oneness where he encountered the divine source of all creation. He described the Core as being suffused with an indescribable presence, which he equated with God, though it was not tied to any specific religious tradition.

In the Core, time and space ceased to exist in the way we understand them. Everything was interconnected, and Dr. Alexander felt as though he had access to universal knowledge. He understood the deeper meaning of life and the interconnectedness of all beings. Questions he had never thought to ask were answered instantaneously, and his prior doubts about spirituality melted away.

He later reflected that the Core was not something that could be fully articulated in human language. Words like "God," "heaven," and "soul" seemed inadequate to describe the profound truths he encountered there.

Dr. Alexander's journey felt timeless, yet eventually, he was guided back. The being of light reassured him that his earthly life still had purpose and that he needed to share what he had learned. Reluctantly, he returned to his physical body, feeling the weight and limitations of human existence once more.

To the astonishment of his medical team, Dr. Alexander awoke from his coma on the seventh day. Even more miraculous was his recovery—despite the severe damage to his brain, he regained full cognitive function within weeks. His survival was deemed medically inexplicable, a case that defied all logic and scientific explanation.

After his recovery, Dr. Alexander was haunted by the memory of the young woman he had encountered in the afterlife. Her presence had been so vivid and significant, yet he had no idea who she was. It wasn't until months later that he discovered her identity.

Through a series of family revelations, Dr. Alexander learned that he had a biological sister he had never met. She had died years before he was adopted. When he saw a photograph of her for the first time, he was stunned—she was the exact woman he had encountered during his NDE.

This discovery cemented his belief in the authenticity of his experience. It wasn't merely a hallucination or a trick of his brain; it was a genuine encounter with a spiritual dimension.

Dr. Alexander's NDE profoundly changed his perspective on consciousness and the nature of reality. No longer a skeptic, he became a vocal advocate for the idea that consciousness exists independently of the brain. He argued that the brain acts as a filter, limiting our awareness in the physical world, but in death, this filter is removed, allowing us to experience the true, boundless nature of existence.

His story resonated deeply with millions of people around the world. He began sharing his insights through lectures, interviews, and his bestselling book, *Proof of Heaven* , which became a cornerstone for discussions about life after death.

Dr. Alexander's journey also reignited the debate about the relationship between science and spirituality. He called for a more open-minded approach to understanding consciousness, urging scientists to explore the mysteries of the mind and its connection to the universe. His experience served as a bridge between the empirical world of science and the transcendent world of spirituality.

Today, Dr. Alexander continues to inspire others with his message of hope and love. He emphasizes that life is a gift, and our experiences—both joyful and painful—are part of a greater tapestry of growth and learning. His story challenges us to reconsider the boundaries of reality and to embrace the possibility that love, connection, and consciousness transcend the physical realm.

Dr. Alexander's NDE is a testament to the transformative power of such experiences. It not only reshaped his life but also encouraged countless others to explore the profound questions of existence: Who are we? What is our purpose? And what awaits us beyond the veil of death?

Howard Storm: From Darkness to Light

Howard Storm's life was a blend of success and skepticism. As a university art professor, he prided himself on intellectual rigor and often dismissed any notion of spirituality or the afterlife. He considered such beliefs as crutches for the weak. Life, to him, was a finite series of experiences defined by what could be proven or observed. That worldview was shattered one fateful day in 1985 when he experienced what he later described as a journey into darkness, despair, and ultimately, redemption.

It began while Howard was leading a student art tour in Paris. He was in his late thirties, thriving in his career and enjoying a comfortable life. During the trip, however, he was struck by excruciating abdominal pain, which quickly turned into a medical emergency. Unbeknownst to him, he had a perforated duodenum—a potentially fatal condition. In a French hospital, he waited for hours in agony, his condition worsening as time slipped away. His wife, Beverly, stayed by his side, helplessly watching as he writhed in pain. Despite her pleas for immediate treatment, hospital staff informed them that no surgeon was available until the next morning.

By the time night fell, Howard's pain had reached an unbearable crescendo, and his body began to shut down. He drifted in and out of consciousness, eventually succumbing to what felt like a final lapse into darkness. Then, something extraordinary happened.

He became acutely aware of standing beside his hospital bed, observing his own body lying lifeless on the mattress. At first, the sight confused him. How could he be outside his body? He felt an eerie clarity, free from the intense pain that had consumed him moments before. Yet, his first reaction wasn't fear but curiosity. He called out to Beverly, but she didn't respond. To his growing frustration, neither did the medical staff bustling around the room. They seemed oblivious to his presence.

As he grappled with this disorienting reality, Howard became aware of voices calling his name. They were distant at first, then grew louder and more distinct. The voices sounded inviting, urging him to follow them. Looking toward the source, he saw shadowy figures at the edge of the room, beckoning him. Intrigued and uncertain, he obeyed.

The figures led him into a gray, featureless void. At first, Howard felt a sense of relief. The pain and chaos of the hospital were gone, replaced by what seemed like a tranquil emptiness. The shadowy figures surrounded him, continuing to coax him forward with soft, persuasive tones. But as they moved deeper into the void, something about them began to change. Their friendly demeanor gave way to hostility. The figures became more aggressive, their voices turning mocking and cruel. They began to jeer at him, their words dripping with malice.

Before long, the jeers escalated into violence. The figures clawed at him, tearing at his flesh and hurling insults. Howard tried to fight back, but his attempts were futile. His assailants seemed to thrive on his despair, feeding off his helplessness. The torment felt eternal, the pain as real as anything he had ever known. He realized he was in a place of utter darkness and hopelessness—a realm devoid of love, light, or redemption. For the first time in his life, Howard confronted the possibility of damnation.

In the depths of this torment, Howard remembered a faint fragment from his childhood: the idea of God. Though he had long rejected religion and dismissed the concept of prayer as superstition, he found himself crying out for help. With nothing left to lose, he whispered the words, "Jesus, save me."

The moment he spoke, an extraordinary light appeared, cutting through the suffocating darkness. The light grew in intensity, radiating warmth, love, and a sense of profound peace. A figure emerged from the light, which Howard later identified as Jesus. This being of pure compassion extended its presence toward him, and Howard felt himself lifted out of the grasp of the shadowy tormentors.

As he floated in the embrace of the light, Howard experienced an overwhelming sense of love. It wasn't the conditional love he had known in life but a boundless, all-encompassing acceptance. He felt every moment of his life being reviewed, not in a way that judged or condemned, but with a perspective that revealed the impact of his actions on others. He saw how his pride, anger, and materialism had created barriers between himself and the people around him. Yet, despite his failings, the light continued to radiate love, as if showing him that redemption was always possible.

Howard was then shown visions of what life could be like if people lived in harmony with divine principles. He saw a world filled with kindness, selflessness, and interconnectedness. The being of light communicated with him, not through words but through a direct transfer of understanding. It was as though the essence of truth was being poured into his very soul.

At one point, Howard was given a choice: to remain in this state of divine love or to return to his earthly body. As much as he longed to stay, the being of light impressed upon him that his journey wasn't finished. There were lessons to be learned and changes to be made. Howard resisted at first, reluctant to leave such a state of peace. But ultimately, he agreed, understanding that his return would serve a greater purpose.

With that decision, Howard felt himself being pulled back toward his body. The warmth and light faded, replaced by the cold reality of the hospital room. He awoke to find himself alive, much to the astonishment of the medical staff. His condition began to improve, and he eventually recovered fully. However, Howard's life was forever changed.

The experience had left him shaken, but also profoundly transformed. The once-proud atheist found himself humbled by the encounter, and his skepticism gave way to a deep faith in God. Howard dedicated the rest of his life to sharing his story, hoping to inspire others to reevaluate their priorities and seek a deeper connection with spirituality.

In the years that followed, Howard became a minister and author, using his testimony to bridge the gap between doubt and faith. His story resonated with thousands, not because it offered easy answers, but because it spoke to the universal longing for meaning, love, and redemption. Howard's journey from darkness to light served as a powerful reminder of the potential for transformation, no matter how far one feels from grace.

Pam Reynolds: Seeing Beyond Death

Pam Reynolds' near-death experience is one of the most remarkable and well-documented cases in modern history, captivating scientists, doctors, and laypeople alike. It occurred in 1991, during a rare and risky surgical procedure known as a "standstill operation," performed to save her life. Pam, a musician from Atlanta, Georgia, had been diagnosed with a giant basilar artery aneurysm at the base of her brain, a condition that posed an imminent threat to her life. The aneurysm was in such a precarious location that conventional surgery was deemed impossible. Instead, her neurosurgeon, Dr. Robert Spetzler, proposed the standstill operation—a procedure that required stopping Pam's heart, draining the blood from her brain, and essentially inducing clinical death to allow the surgical team to operate without risking rupture.

The procedure was daunting, but Pam agreed. She had no idea that her experience would become a cornerstone in the study of near-death phenomena.

On the day of the surgery, Pam was brought into the operating room and placed under general anesthesia. Her body was cooled to 60 degrees Fahrenheit, her heartbeat and brain activity were stopped, and her blood was drained. By all medical standards, Pam was clinically dead—her brain had ceased functioning, her heart was no longer beating, and her body was incapable of independent life. For all intents and purposes, Pam Reynolds was as close to death as one could be while still having a chance to return.

Yet, it was during this time of profound inactivity that Pam would later describe a vivid, extraordinary journey—a journey that would defy conventional understanding of life and consciousness.

Pam's experience began with the sensation of leaving her body. She described feeling herself lift out of her physical form, rising above the operating table. From this elevated vantage point, she could see the surgical team working on her body. She recounted observing the medical instruments being used, particularly a bone saw. She noted its peculiar appearance, likening it to an electric toothbrush. This was an astonishing detail, as Pam's eyes were taped shut and she had no prior knowledge of the tools involved in the surgery. Furthermore, her auditory perception during this state was equally inexplicable. Despite her ears being plugged and covered to monitor auditory brainstem responses, Pam claimed to hear conversations among the surgeons. She later recounted specific comments, including one doctor's remark about the difficulty of accessing her femoral artery due to its small size.

As the surgery progressed, Pam felt herself being drawn toward a radiant, golden light. The light was accompanied by a sense of profound peace and love, unlike anything she had ever known. She described this feeling as being enveloped in unconditional warmth, free from fear, pain, or judgment. It was a state of existence that transcended earthly comprehension, a realm where love was the fundamental essence. As she moved closer to the light, Pam became aware of the presence of spiritual beings. Though she could not identify them by name, she felt an intrinsic connection to these entities, as though they were family or loved ones. They communicated with her, not through words, but through a direct transfer of thought and understanding.

At one point, Pam felt herself being guided through what she described as a tunnel. The tunnel was dark yet comforting, and at its end was the source of the light—a place she intuitively understood to be a realm of pure consciousness. Pam felt herself expanding, her awareness growing boundless as she merged with this radiant presence. In this state, she experienced a profound understanding of life, love, and the interconnectedness of all things. Time and space ceased to exist; everything was happening simultaneously, and Pam felt an overwhelming sense of unity with the universe.

However, her journey was not to last. The spiritual beings communicated to her that it was not yet her time, and that she had to return to her body. Pam resisted. She did not want to leave this place of serenity and unconditional love. She pleaded to stay, but the beings insisted, reminding her of responsibilities and unfinished purposes in her earthly life. With that, Pam felt herself being pulled back into her body. She described the return as abrupt and jarring, like being plunged into icy water. The physical pain and heaviness of her earthly form were stark contrasts to the ethereal freedom she had just experienced.

When Pam awoke after the surgery, she began recounting her experience. Initially, the medical team was skeptical. However, when Pam began providing specific details about the operation—details she could not have known due to her state of clinical death—the skepticism turned to astonishment. She described the bone saw, the conversations among the surgeons, and even the music playing in the operating room, which she identified as "Hotel California" by the Eagles. These details were later corroborated by the surgical team, lending credibility to her account.

Pam's case quickly gained attention from researchers and scientists studying near-death experiences. It was particularly compelling because of the controlled conditions of her surgery. During the standstill operation, Pam's brain was completely inactive. Electroencephalogram (EEG) monitoring confirmed a flatline, indicating no neural activity. Her body temperature was reduced to a point where metabolic functions ceased, and her heart was stopped. Under such conditions, conventional science held that consciousness should have been impossible. Yet, Pam's vivid and detailed experience suggested otherwise, challenging prevailing assumptions about the relationship between the brain and consciousness.

Pam Reynolds' story has become a cornerstone in the field of near-death studies. It has been cited in numerous books, articles, and documentaries exploring the nature of consciousness and the possibility of life beyond death. For many, her account offers hope and reassurance, suggesting that death is not an end but a transition to a different state of existence. For skeptics, her experience raises questions about the limits of scientific understanding and the potential for unexplored dimensions of human consciousness.

Pam herself emerged from the experience transformed. She described a newfound appreciation for life, a deeper sense of purpose, and a diminished fear of death. She often spoke about the profound peace and love she felt during her journey, emphasizing the importance of living authentically and cherishing every moment. Her story continues to inspire and intrigue, serving as a testament to the mysteries of life, death, and the uncharted territories of human consciousness.

Don Piper: Ninety Minutes in Eternity

The day was cold and unremarkable when Don Piper set off on a trip that would change his life forever. A pastor by profession, he had been attending a church conference in Texas and was on his way home, driving across a long stretch of road bordered by dense woods. It was the kind of highway that stretched endlessly into the horizon, a place where the hum of the tires and the rhythm of passing mile markers became a sort of meditative lull. Don had no idea that in just a few moments, his life as he knew it would be violently interrupted.

As Don approached a narrow bridge, he spotted an 18-wheeler coming from the opposite direction. He didn't think much of it at first—large trucks on these roads were as common as the endless trees. But in a split second, the massive truck veered into his lane. Don had no time to react. The collision was catastrophic, the truck crushing his Ford Escort like a tin can. First responders who arrived at the scene found his car mangled beyond recognition. The dashboard was pushed into his chest, his legs pinned under the crumpled metal, and his body unnaturally still. After checking for a pulse, paramedics declared him dead.

His body was covered with a tarp as emergency workers tended to others involved in the accident. Traffic backed up for miles as drivers slowed to catch a glimpse of the devastation. For over an hour, Don lay lifeless in his crushed vehicle. But unbeknownst to those around him, Don was no longer aware of the wreckage or the chaos. He was somewhere else entirely.

Don's first sensation was not fear or pain but an overwhelming sense of peace. It was as if every worry, every ounce of earthly concern, had melted away. He was standing before a magnificent gate, unlike anything he had ever seen. The gate shimmered with an unearthly light, its beauty both majestic and inviting. It was made of a substance that seemed to defy description, something like pearl but alive, radiating a warmth that felt like home. Music filled the air—ethereal, harmonious melodies that transcended any earthly symphony. The sound wrapped around him, each note a cascade of love and joy.

As Don stood there, marveling at the gates, he noticed figures approaching. They were familiar, yet at first, he couldn't quite place them. Then, one by one, he recognized them—they were loved ones who had passed away. His grandfather was there, smiling warmly, his features as vivid and youthful as Don had remembered from childhood. There was a friend who had died in a tragic accident, his face beaming with happiness. The longer Don looked, the more faces he saw—each one someone who had played a meaningful role in his life, their presence a testament to the love and connections that had defined his time on Earth.

The reunion was unlike anything Don could have imagined. There were no tears, no regrets, only pure joy and the unshakable certainty that he was exactly where he was meant to be. The people surrounding him embraced him, their touch imbued with an indescribable sense of comfort. They didn't speak in words, yet he understood them perfectly. Their love was a tangible force, enveloping him in a way that made every earthly sorrow seem insignificant. It was then that Don realized he was in heaven.

Every detail of the place seemed designed to evoke awe and wonder. The colors were richer, more vibrant than anything he had seen on Earth, as though the very air was alive with light. The streets were paved with what appeared to be gold, yet it wasn't cold or metallic; it was warm and inviting, glowing softly under his feet. The atmosphere was charged with love—a love so profound that it seemed to emanate from every molecule around him. It was a place without pain, without fear, without the burdens of a mortal existence. Don felt whole in a way he had never thought possible.

But as he basked in this heavenly peace, something began to change. Don felt a tugging sensation, faint at first but growing stronger. It was as though he were being drawn away from the gates, pulled back toward a place he had no desire to return to. He resisted, wanting to stay in this perfect realm, but the pull was unrelenting. He became aware of a voice—a distant prayer. The voice was soft but insistent, growing louder with each passing moment. It wasn't a voice he recognized, but he could feel its urgency. Someone was praying for him.

Back on Earth, a pastor named Dick Onerecker had arrived at the scene of the accident. As he surveyed the wreckage, he felt an unshakable conviction that he needed to pray for Don, even though the paramedics had declared him dead. Dick climbed into the wreckage, maneuvering around the crushed metal to lay a hand on Don's lifeless body. He began to pray aloud, asking God to restore Don's life. The words were simple but fervent, an act of faith in a situation that seemed utterly hopeless.

As Dick prayed, Don suddenly became aware of his body again. It was a shocking transition—from the peace and beauty of heaven to the pain and brokenness of Earth. The contrast was staggering. He opened his eyes to find himself trapped in the twisted remains of his car, his body wracked with pain. The paramedics, who had long since moved on to other tasks, were stunned to find him alive. The tarp was pulled back, and a flurry of activity ensued as they worked to extricate him from the wreckage.

Don's recovery was long and arduous. His injuries were severe, requiring multiple surgeries and months of rehabilitation. Yet, despite the physical pain, Don carried with him the unshakable memory of what he had experienced. He spoke of heaven with a clarity and conviction that left no room for doubt. The love, the peace, the music—it was all as vivid in his mind as it had been in the moment. The experience transformed him, deepening his faith and giving him a renewed sense of purpose.

He began sharing his story, not for fame or recognition, but because he felt called to do so. People from all walks of life were drawn to his testimony, finding comfort and hope in his account of heaven. Don's message was simple yet profound: there is a life beyond this one, a place of unimaginable beauty and love. And while his journey to that place had been unexpected and uninvited, it had given him a glimpse of eternity that he would carry with him forever.

Even years later, Don's experience continues to resonate with those who hear it. For some, it is a source of spiritual inspiration; for others, it is a reminder to cherish the time they have on Earth. For Don, it is a constant affirmation of the power of faith, love, and the unbreakable bond between heaven and Earth.

(This retelling captures the essence of Don Piper's near-death experience as detailed in his book, *90 Minutes in Heaven*.)

Colton Burpo: A Child's Journey to Heaven

It was the spring of 2003 when Colton Burpo, a lively and spirited four-year-old boy from Imperial, Nebraska, faced a health crisis that would change his family's life forever. Colton was the son of Todd and Sonja Burpo, a deeply religious couple. Todd was a pastor, and Sonja was a devoted mother who spent her days caring for their children. They were an ordinary family, living in a tight-knit community, where faith played a central role in their lives. However, nothing could have prepared them for the extraordinary events that would unfold.

It all began with what seemed like a routine illness. Colton complained of stomach pain and began vomiting, leading his parents to think it was the flu. But his symptoms didn't improve, and within days, he was so ill that Todd and Sonja knew something was gravely wrong. They rushed him to the hospital, where doctors quickly discovered the problem: Colton's appendix had burst, causing a severe infection to spread throughout his tiny body. The situation was critical, and surgery was the only option.

The hours leading up to Colton's surgery were agonizing for his parents. Todd, already under immense stress from a series of personal setbacks, including a broken leg and financial struggles, was at his breaking point. He found solace in prayer, asking God to save his son. Sonja, too, clung to her faith, though her worry was almost unbearable. The sight of Colton, pale and weak, lying in a hospital bed with wires and tubes attached to his small body, left her heartbroken.

When Colton was taken into the operating room, the Burpos were consumed by fear and doubt. They knew the surgery was risky and that there was no guarantee of success. As they waited in the sterile hospital corridor, time seemed to crawl. Todd tried to maintain a facade of strength, but inside, he was pleading with God for a miracle.

Hours later, the surgeon emerged to deliver the news. The operation had been successful, but Colton was not out of danger. His recovery would be long and uncertain. Relieved but still on edge, Todd and Sonja sat by Colton's bedside, watching over him as he began to heal. Slowly, he regained strength, and within a few weeks, the worst seemed to be behind them.

Life started to return to normal, or so they thought. Colton resumed his playful, energetic ways, bringing joy and laughter back into the Burpo household. But then, a series of strange remarks from their young son began to unsettle Todd and Sonja. It started innocently enough, with Colton casually mentioning things that he couldn't possibly have known.

One day, as the family was driving past the hospital, Colton said, "That's where the angels sang to me." His parents exchanged puzzled looks. Todd asked what he meant, and Colton described how, during his surgery, he had left his body and gone to heaven. He spoke with the innocence and clarity of a child, recounting vivid details of a realm filled with light, music, and indescribable beauty.

Colton described seeing angels and meeting Jesus, whom he recognized instantly. "Jesus has a rainbow horse," he said matter-of-factly, adding that he sat on Jesus' lap while the angels sang to him. He also mentioned meeting family members who had passed away, including his great-grandfather, Pop, who had died long before Colton was born. Colton spoke about Pop with such familiarity that Todd and Sonja were stunned. The boy described details about Pop's life that no one had shared with him.

The most astonishing moment came when Colton mentioned meeting a little girl in heaven. She told him she was his sister. This revelation left Sonja in tears. Years earlier, she had suffered a miscarriage, a painful loss they had never discussed with Colton. Yet he described the girl with uncanny accuracy, saying she had dark hair and looked like her mother. "She said she couldn't wait to meet you," Colton told Sonja.

Todd and Sonja struggled to process what they were hearing. As devout Christians, they believed in heaven, but Colton's detailed account of his experience went beyond anything they could have imagined. They asked him questions, trying to understand, but Colton's answers were always consistent. He spoke with confidence and sincerity, never wavering in his descriptions of what he had seen.

Colton's stories spread through their community, sparking awe and curiosity. Some people were skeptical, dismissing his account as a child's imagination. Others were deeply moved, seeing his experience as proof of the divine. Todd decided to share their family's story, believing it could bring hope to others. Together, he and Sonja wrote *Heaven is for Real* , a book that detailed Colton's journey and the profound impact it had on their lives.

The book became a phenomenon, resonating with readers around the world. Many found comfort in Colton's words, feeling reassured about the existence of heaven and the promise of an afterlife. For the Burpos, the experience strengthened their faith and deepened their understanding of God's love.

Colton's near-death experience was not just a story of survival but also a testament to the power of hope and the mysteries of the spiritual realm. His innocent perspective reminded people of the beauty of childlike faith and the possibility of miracles. Though the skeptics remained, the Burpos were unwavering in their belief that Colton had indeed glimpsed heaven. For them, his experience was a gift, a glimpse into eternity that brought peace and purpose to their lives.

As the years passed, Colton grew older, but he never forgot what he had seen. His story continued to inspire, touching the hearts of countless individuals who longed for reassurance about the afterlife. For Todd and Sonja, it was a reminder that even in their darkest moments, they were not alone. Through their son's incredible journey, they found a renewed sense of hope and a profound connection to the divine.

Colton's tale remains one of the most compelling and widely discussed near-death experiences of our time. It is a story of faith, love, and the enduring power of a child's innocent testimony to bring light into a world often shadowed by doubt. For the Burpos, and for many who have heard Colton's account, it is a powerful affirmation that heaven is, indeed, for real.

Vicki Noratuk: The Blind Woman Who "Saw" During Her NDE

Vicki was born blind. Her world was one of sound, touch, and scent—a rich tapestry of sensations that she had woven together throughout her life to navigate a sightless existence. She had no visual references to anchor her reality. Colors, light, and shapes were concepts she understood only through the descriptions of others. She lived in a world defined by the subtle vibrations of footsteps, the gentle whispers of wind, and the warmth of a loved one's embrace.

At 22 years old, Vicki's life took an unexpected turn. She was involved in a severe car accident that left her body gravely injured. Rushed to the hospital, she was in critical condition. As doctors and nurses worked frantically to stabilize her, Vicki's consciousness began to fade. Then, suddenly, everything shifted.

In an instant, she became acutely aware of leaving her body. She floated upward, weightless and free. She didn't feel pain or fear—only curiosity and an unshakable sense of peace. For the first time, she could see. It was a sensation so unfamiliar, yet so natural, that it overwhelmed her. She looked down and realized she was hovering above the emergency room. Below her, she saw her own body lying on the operating table. Doctors and nurses moved with purpose, their faces etched with focus and concern.

She saw the crash cart being pushed in and heard one of the doctors call for defibrillator pads. The shock paddles were pressed against her chest, sending electrical currents through her body in a desperate attempt to restart her heart. Vicki noticed the doctor's glasses slipping down his nose and the nurse adjusting the straps on her gown. These were details she could not have known. And yet, she saw them with absolute clarity.

Vicki's newfound vision wasn't limited to the physical details of the room. She perceived emotions emanating from the people around her—a blend of urgency, anxiety, and hope. Their thoughts seemed to ripple outward, forming patterns she could almost touch. It was as if she had tapped into an entirely different dimension of existence.

Her focus shifted, and she felt herself being drawn toward a tunnel. It wasn't a dark or foreboding space but a luminous passage that radiated warmth and love. At the far end, a brilliant light beckoned her. She couldn't resist its pull; it was as though her soul recognized the light as home. As she moved through the tunnel, she felt an overwhelming sense of serenity. The pain, fear, and limitations she had known in her earthly life melted away.

When she emerged into the light, she found herself in a place that defied description. It wasn't bound by the physical laws she had always understood. Colors pulsed with life, shimmering and shifting in ways she had never imagined. It was as if the very air hummed with joy and harmony. She could feel the love of the universe enveloping her, a profound connection that transcended words.

In this realm, she encountered beings of light. They didn't have distinct forms but exuded personalities that she intuitively recognized. They communicated with her, not through words but through thoughts and emotions that flowed directly into her mind. These beings seemed to radiate wisdom and compassion. They reassured her, telling her she was deeply loved and that her journey was far from over.

Vicki felt her spirit expand. She began to see the interconnectedness of all things. Every action, every thought, every emotion seemed to ripple outward, touching the lives of others in ways she had never comprehended. The universe, she realized, was a web of infinite connections, each thread shimmering with purpose and meaning.

The beings guided her to a reflective space where she was shown scenes from her life—not as fragmented memories but as a cohesive narrative. She saw moments of joy and pain, triumph and struggle. She understood how every experience had shaped her and how even her blindness had been a gift, teaching her resilience, empathy, and the ability to appreciate the non-visual beauty of the world.

Then, she was shown a glimpse of what lay ahead if she chose to return to her earthly life. She saw herself embracing her family, sharing her story, and inspiring others with her insights. She understood that her NDE was not an end but a beginning—a chance to bring hope and wisdom to those around her.

Vicki wasn't ready to leave this place of boundless love and light, but she knew her journey wasn't over. The beings gently told her it wasn't her time. She felt herself being drawn back through the tunnel, away from the brilliance and harmony of the light. As she approached her physical body, the sensation of weight and limitation began to return. It was like slipping into a heavy suit after being free.

When she opened her eyes, she was back in the hospital. The world around her was dark again, her blindness restored. But something fundamental had changed. She carried within her the memory of her experience—the vivid colors, the profound peace, and the unconditional love she had felt.

As she recovered, Vicki shared her story with friends, family, and eventually researchers studying near-death experiences. They were stunned by the details she described. She accurately recounted the equipment in the operating room, the actions of the medical staff, and even the precise conversations they had—all things she couldn't have known without the ability to see. Her account became a cornerstone case in NDE research, challenging the understanding of consciousness and sensory perception.

For Vicki, the experience wasn't just an extraordinary event; it was a transformation. She returned to life with a renewed sense of purpose and an unshakable belief in the interconnectedness of all things. Though she couldn't see in the physical sense, she felt she had been given a vision far greater than sight—the ability to perceive the beauty, love, and unity that underpins existence.

Through her story, Vicki inspired countless others, offering hope to those who feared death and a reminder to cherish the life they had. She proved that even in darkness, there is light. And even in blindness, there is vision.

Dr. Mary Neal: Between Two Worlds

D r. Mary Neal's story is one of profound transformation and a deep connection to the spiritual realm. An orthopedic surgeon by trade, Neal was a pragmatic, logical thinker, accustomed to the clinical world of medicine and science. Yet, her life changed irrevocably during a kayaking trip in Chile, where she experienced a near-death event that challenged everything she thought she knew about existence, faith, and purpose.

In the year 1999, Neal, an experienced kayaker, embarked on an adventurous trip to South America with her husband and a group of friends. The rivers of Chile were known for their thrilling rapids, and this journey was meant to be an exciting escape from their busy lives. Neal was particularly skilled in navigating turbulent waters, but on this fateful day, the unexpected happened. As they approached a treacherous section of the river, her kayak was sucked into a powerful waterfall, trapping her underneath.

The force of the water was overwhelming, pinning her against submerged rocks. Despite her efforts to free herself, she couldn't move. She was trapped, her body pressed by the relentless torrent of water, and she soon realized that escape was impossible. As the moments stretched into minutes, she began to lose her grip on consciousness. A sense of panic gave way to a calm acceptance as she resigned herself to the reality that she was drowning.

It was then that Neal's world shifted. She later described feeling her spirit separate from her body, a sensation of weightlessness and detachment. She was no longer aware of the water pressing against her or the struggle of her physical body. Instead, she found herself in a realm that defied earthly description, a place suffused with an overwhelming sense of peace and love.

Neal recalled being surrounded by spiritual beings, whom she identified as angels or divine entities. These beings radiated an immense warmth and familiarity, as though they had known her for eternity. They were dressed in robes of light, shimmering with a brilliance that seemed alive. Neal felt no fear, only an unshakable sense of comfort and belonging. The beings communicated with her, though not with words; their messages were conveyed directly to her mind, a form of pure, unfiltered understanding.

As she floated in this ethereal realm, Neal was overcome by a profound sense of unconditional love. She described it as a love so pure and complete that it transcended anything she had ever experienced on Earth. She felt entirely embraced by this love, and it filled her with a peace that was beyond comprehension. In this state, Neal became acutely aware of the interconnectedness of all things. She understood that life on Earth was but a fragment of a much larger reality, one that was beautiful, eternal, and divinely orchestrated.

During her time in this realm, Neal had a life review—not a judgment, but a loving reflection on her earthly experiences. She saw her life from a new perspective, one that highlighted the ways her actions had rippled through the lives of others. She was shown that even the smallest acts of kindness had profound significance, and she felt immense gratitude for the lessons her life had taught her.

Then, Neal was shown glimpses of the future. Among these revelations was the knowledge that her eldest son, then only a young boy, would die at a young age. The news was devastating, even in this heavenly realm, but she was given the assurance that his death would serve a greater purpose and that he would be deeply cared for in the afterlife. This foreknowledge, though heartbreaking, was imparted with an understanding that all things unfolded according to a divine plan.

Neal felt no desire to return to her earthly body. She was content to remain in this realm of peace and love, but the spiritual beings informed her that her time was not yet complete. They told her that she still had work to do on Earth, a purpose that required her to return. Though she resisted, she was gently but firmly guided back toward her physical body.

At that moment, Neal became aware of her earthly surroundings again. Her friends had been frantically trying to rescue her. After nearly 15 minutes underwater, they managed to pull her lifeless body from the river. They began performing CPR, and against all odds, Neal's heart began to beat. She was alive, though her body was battered and broken. Her lungs were filled with water, her legs were severely injured, and she was rushed to a hospital for treatment.

The recovery process was long and arduous. Neal endured multiple surgeries and months of rehabilitation. However, she emerged from the experience a changed person. The memory of her time in the spiritual realm remained vivid, and it transformed her perspective on life and death. She no longer feared death, seeing it as a transition to a state of unimaginable beauty and love.

Neal also felt a renewed sense of purpose. She began sharing her story, despite initial hesitation. As a doctor, she was acutely aware of the skepticism she might face, but she felt compelled to spread the message of hope and love that she had received. Her account resonated with many, offering comfort to those facing grief or struggling with questions about the afterlife.

Years later, the prophecy about her son came to pass. Her eldest child died in a tragic accident, just as she had been shown during her near-death experience. While the loss was excruciating, Neal found solace in the knowledge that her son was in the same realm of love and peace she had experienced. She drew strength from her faith and the certainty that they would one day be reunited.

Dr. Mary Neal's story continues to inspire countless individuals. Her near-death experience is not only a testament to the power of love and connection but also a reminder of the profound mystery of existence. For Neal, the lessons of her journey are clear: life is precious, interconnected, and imbued with purpose. Her account has become a beacon of hope for those seeking answers about life's greatest questions, offering a glimpse into a reality that transcends the physical world.

Mellen-Thomas Benedict : Journey Through the Light and Back

Mellen-Thomas Benedict's near-death experience is one of the most profound and detailed accounts ever recorded, a tale of transformation, cosmic insight, and unexpected survival. Diagnosed with terminal brain cancer in 1982, Mellen was told he had only a few months to live. Faced with the inevitability of death, he plunged into despair, grappling with questions about life's meaning and his place in the universe. Yet, what began as his darkest hour turned into an extraordinary journey that would not only change his life but challenge the very fabric of how we understand consciousness and existence.

Mellen's life before his diagnosis had been marked by disillusionment. He was an artist by profession, but his thoughts were consumed by the growing environmental crises and the seeming futility of humanity's struggles. He felt hopeless about the world's future and carried this despair into his dying days. When his condition worsened, Mellen prepared for the end. He refused chemotherapy and instead opted to die peacefully at home. On a fateful morning, knowing his time was near, he asked to be left alone. He lay on his bed, surrendering to what he thought was the final moment of his existence. What followed, however, was far from the oblivion he had expected.

As Mellen's consciousness began to fade, he felt himself detach from his body. There was no pain, only a sense of release. He described an awareness of floating above his physical form, observing the room around him with remarkable clarity. He could see his body lying still on the bed, and though he recognized it as his, he felt no attachment to it. This state of detached awareness quickly gave way to an extraordinary phenomenon: a brilliant light appeared, drawing him toward it with an irresistible pull. This was no ordinary light; it was alive, pulsating with warmth, love, and intelligence. Mellen felt enveloped by it, as though every fiber of his being was being bathed in unconditional love.

As he moved closer to the light, Mellen realized it was communicating with him, not through words but through an intimate, all-encompassing understanding. He referred to it as "the Light of God," though he emphasized that it was not bound to any particular religion or belief system. The Light seemed to understand every question he had ever pondered and offered answers that transcended human language. It was here that Mellen's journey truly began.

The Light, he explained, asked him if he was ready to die. Mellen, filled with awe and curiosity, responded that he wanted to understand more about life and the universe before letting go. The Light agreed, and what followed was an astonishing journey through what Mellen described as the fabric of creation itself. He was shown the entirety of his life in a vivid, panoramic review. Every moment, every decision, and every interaction was replayed, not as a series of disconnected memories, but as a cohesive tapestry that revealed the interconnectedness of all things. He felt the emotions of those he had affected, both positively and negatively, gaining a deep understanding of the consequences of his actions.

The life review was not judgmental. Instead, it was a learning experience. The Light radiated unconditional love, showing Mellen that even his mistakes were valuable opportunities for growth. This revelation filled him with an overwhelming sense of peace. For the first time, he understood that life was not about achieving perfection but about evolving through experiences.

After the life review, the Light invited Mellen to journey further. He was transported beyond earthly concerns, beyond the confines of time and space, into what he described as "the Void." This was not a dark, empty nothingness but a womb of creation, a space teeming with potential. It was here that Mellen said he encountered the origin of all things—the point where consciousness itself emerges. In the Void, he understood that all life is interconnected, a part of an infinite cycle of energy and love. He saw that humanity, despite its flaws, was an essential expression of this universal consciousness, constantly evolving toward greater awareness.

From the Void, Mellen was shown the workings of the universe in a way that defied human comprehension. He described seeing the Earth from a cosmic perspective, its beauty and fragility illuminated by the Light. He understood the intricate balance of nature and the importance of humanity's role as stewards of the planet. He also glimpsed into what he called "future probabilities," potential timelines for humanity based on collective choices. While some of these visions were troubling, he was filled with hope, as the Light assured him that love and creativity were powerful forces capable of transforming even the darkest scenarios.

At one point, Mellen was given the choice to continue his journey into the afterlife or return to his earthly body. Though he felt an almost unbearable longing to stay in the presence of the Light, he realized there was still more for him to do in the physical world. He was filled with a renewed sense of purpose and a desire to share the insights he had gained. With that decision, the journey began to reverse. He felt himself being gently guided back to his body, the Light's presence lingering with him as he re-entered his physical form.

When Mellen awoke, he was profoundly changed. He described feeling as though he had been "reprogrammed." His despair and fear were replaced with an unshakable sense of peace and love. Even more astonishing was the fact that his terminal cancer appeared to have vanished. Doctors were baffled by his recovery, unable to explain how a man so close to death could return not only healed but rejuvenated. Mellen attributed his miraculous recovery to the transformative power of the Light.

In the years that followed, Mellen dedicated his life to sharing his experience and the insights he gained. He became a speaker and researcher, exploring the intersection of science, spirituality, and human potential. He emphasized that his experience was not about promoting any specific religion but about understanding the universal truths that connect all of humanity. His message was one of hope: that love, creativity, and consciousness are the building blocks of existence, and that every individual has the power to contribute to the betterment of the world.

Mellen's story continues to inspire and challenge people from all walks of life. His journey through the Light and back offers a glimpse into the profound mysteries of existence, reminding us of the boundless potential of the human spirit and the enduring power of love. Whether seen as a spiritual revelation, a neurological phenomenon, or something beyond explanation, Mellen-Thomas Benedict's near-death experience remains a testament to the transformative power of facing death —and choosing life.

George Ritchie: The Christmas Eve Journey

On a cold night in December 1943, George Ritchie, a 20-year-old Army private stationed at Camp Barkeley, Texas, was struck down by a severe case of double pneumonia. With antibiotics like penicillin not yet widely available, pneumonia was often a death sentence. Ritchie had been preparing to train as a doctor, but on this fateful night, his aspirations were cut short when his condition worsened dramatically, and he lost consciousness.

As he later described, this was not the end of his life but the beginning of an extraordinary journey that would forever alter his understanding of life, death, and the nature of existence itself.

Ritchie's first awareness after losing consciousness was an unusual sense of clarity. He found himself sitting up in his hospital bed, feeling perfectly healthy and energetic. Confused, he looked around and saw his own lifeless body lying beneath the sheets. The sight was shocking—how could he be both here, alive and alert, and there, apparently dead? He realized with a jolt that he had somehow separated from his physical form.

Panicking, Ritchie thought of his upcoming military appointment in Richmond, Virginia. He needed to leave immediately. Without understanding how, he suddenly found himself flying through the air, faster than anything he had ever imagined. The sensation was exhilarating but bewildering. As he sped toward Richmond, he noticed he was no longer bound by physical limitations. He could pass through walls and barriers effortlessly. Yet, something felt strange—everything seemed devoid of life, muted, and shadowy.

When Ritchie arrived in Richmond, he searched for familiar landmarks. He spotted a soda shop he had visited before but was surprised to find it completely empty. There were no people, no activity, only silence. It was as though the city had been frozen in time. Increasingly disoriented, Ritchie began to wonder if he had truly died and what this ghostly experience meant.

Then, as suddenly as he had arrived, Ritchie felt himself being pulled back. He was no longer traveling alone but was accompanied by a radiant, all-encompassing light. The light was unlike anything he had ever seen—brighter than the sun yet gentle, comforting, and alive. Within it, Ritchie perceived the presence of a being of immense power and love. Although he later referred to this being as Jesus, he emphasized that it was not the religious figure he had imagined growing up. Instead, it was a presence that emanated unconditional love, understanding, and peace.

The being of light did not speak in words but communicated directly to Ritchie's mind in a way that felt deeply personal and profound. Ritchie was immediately enveloped in an overwhelming sense of acceptance. All his fears and doubts melted away in the presence of this loving intelligence.

As the light surrounded him, Ritchie's life began to play out before him in a vivid, panoramic review. Every moment of his existence unfolded in intricate detail—not just his actions, but their consequences, the emotions they elicited in others, and the ripple effects they caused. He saw moments of kindness and cruelty, of love and selfishness, and was able to experience them from multiple perspectives. He felt the pain he had caused others, as well as the joy he had brought into their lives.

What struck Ritchie most was the complete absence of judgment from the being of light. There was no condemnation or punishment, only a deep and compassionate understanding of his humanity. Ritchie realized that the purpose of the review was not to shame him but to teach him about the importance of love, kindness, and self-awareness. Every small act of love, he was shown, carried a far greater significance than he had ever imagined.

After the life review, the being of light invited Ritchie to journey further. What followed was an exploration of realms that he described as beyond anything he had ever conceived. He was taken to various dimensions, each revealing profound truths about life and the universe. In one realm, he observed people who appeared trapped in a state of disconnection and despair. These individuals seemed unaware of the radiant light surrounding them, consumed instead by their own thoughts and desires. Ritchie understood that this was not a punishment but a reflection of their internal state—a self-created isolation from the divine.

In another realm, Ritchie encountered beings who radiated love and wisdom. These beings seemed to be engaged in acts of learning, creating, and helping others. He felt that this realm was closer to the presence of the being of light and represented a higher state of spiritual growth. The love and harmony in this dimension were indescribable, and Ritchie felt a deep longing to remain there.

However, the being of light communicated that Ritchie's journey was not yet complete. He was shown the Earth from a cosmic perspective, witnessing its beauty and fragility. He saw humanity's interconnectedness and the critical role of love and compassion in shaping the future. Ritchie was filled with awe as he realized that every individual's actions contributed to the greater whole. The message was clear: life was not random but profoundly meaningful, and every person had a unique purpose.

Ritchie's journey culminated in an encounter with what he described as the source of all creation—a boundless, infinite presence that defied description. In this presence, he felt completely united with everything that existed, a part of an eternal and loving consciousness. This moment of oneness was the pinnacle of his experience, leaving him with a deep understanding of the divine nature of life.

Despite his yearning to stay in this state of bliss, Ritchie was told he needed to return to his earthly life. He protested, not wanting to leave the peace and love he had found, but the being of light reassured him that his time on Earth was not yet finished. There was work for him to do, lessons to share, and a purpose to fulfill. Reluctantly, Ritchie agreed and found himself drawn back to his body.

When he awoke in the hospital, Ritchie was disoriented and overwhelmed by what he had experienced. To the astonishment of the medical staff, he was alive—though his condition had been so dire that he had been declared clinically dead for nine minutes. Over time, Ritchie processed his journey and came to understand its profound implications. His experience left him with an unshakable conviction in the power of love and the interconnectedness of all life.

Ritchie went on to fulfill his dream of becoming a doctor, dedicating his life to helping others and sharing the insights he had gained. He wrote about his near-death experience in his book *Return from Tomorrow* , which has inspired countless readers and researchers to explore the mysteries of consciousness and the afterlife.

The Christmas Eve journey of George Ritchie remains one of the most compelling accounts of a near-death experience, offering a powerful reminder that life is a sacred gift filled with meaning, purpose, and opportunities for growth. Through his story, Ritchie invites us to reconsider our priorities, embrace love and compassion, and recognize the divine presence that connects us all.

Betty Eadie: Embraced by the Light

Betty Eadie's story begins in 1973 when she was admitted to the hospital for a routine hysterectomy. A wife and mother of seven, Betty was 31 years old and lived a seemingly ordinary life. Yet what unfolded during this medical procedure would profoundly alter her perception of existence, offering her a glimpse of a world that was anything but ordinary. During her recovery from surgery, Betty experienced what she initially thought was a dream. But as the moments unfolded, she realized it was something far more significant—a near-death experience that would forever change her life and inspire millions of others.

As she drifted off to sleep that evening in her hospital bed, Betty suddenly found herself leaving her physical body. She described the sensation as light, effortless, and deeply peaceful. Looking back, she saw her body lying motionless on the hospital bed and felt no fear or attachment to it. Instead, she felt a sense of curiosity and wonder as she realized she was still very much alive, though no longer bound by her physical form.

Before she had time to process what was happening, Betty became aware of three beings standing near her bed. These beings radiated an indescribable love and warmth, and she immediately felt a deep connection to them. Though she couldn't recall ever meeting them in life, they felt familiar, as though they had always been with her. They reassured her with their presence, and she felt completely safe in their company.

The beings of light communicated with Betty, not through words, but through thoughts and emotions. They told her it was time to leave, and together they ascended into a realm of astonishing beauty. Betty described moving through a tunnel filled with a soft, radiant light that seemed to pulse with life. At the end of the tunnel, she was greeted by a presence she identified as Jesus Christ, though she emphasized that the love and acceptance radiating from this being were universal and not confined to any specific religion. In His presence, she felt completely known, as though every detail of her life and soul was understood—and loved unconditionally.

Betty experienced a panoramic life review in which every moment of her existence was laid bare, not as a judgment, but as an opportunity to learn and grow. She felt the emotions of those she had affected, both positively and negatively, and gained a profound understanding of how her choices had rippled outward. She realized that even small acts of kindness carried immense significance and that the central purpose of life was to love and serve others.

After the life review, Betty was shown a realm of indescribable beauty. She described fields of vibrant colors unlike anything on Earth, filled with flowers and trees that seemed to exude a life force of their own. Everything in this realm was alive and interconnected, radiating a deep harmony and peace. She met other spiritual beings who seemed to be engaged in various activities, learning, creating, and growing. Betty felt an overwhelming sense of belonging in this place, as though she had finally come home.

During her journey, Betty was given profound insights into the nature of the universe and the purpose of life. She was shown that every soul has a unique mission on Earth, a role to play in the grand tapestry of creation. She learned that challenges and hardships, while difficult, are opportunities for spiritual growth and development. She also received knowledge about the interconnectedness of all life, understanding that humanity, nature, and the cosmos are deeply interwoven.

Betty's experience was not confined to lofty spiritual revelations. She was also shown practical truths about everyday life. She understood the importance of gratitude, forgiveness, and love in shaping our reality. She realized that many of life's difficulties stem from our disconnection from these principles and that reconnecting with love and gratitude could transform not only individual lives but the world as a whole.

Despite the overwhelming peace and joy she felt in this realm, Betty was told it was not yet her time to stay. Her purpose on Earth was not yet fulfilled, and she was given the choice to return. Though she longed to remain in the presence of such unconditional love, she knew she had to go back to complete her mission. She was assured that she would carry the memory of this experience with her and that it would guide her in fulfilling her life's purpose.

Returning to her body was a painful and disorienting process. Betty described feeling a heavy weight as she re-entered her physical form, accompanied by the limitations and frailties of earthly life. Yet, as she awoke in her hospital bed, she carried a profound sense of peace and purpose. She knew she had been given a gift—not just for herself, but to share with others.

The aftermath of Betty's near-death experience was transformative. Her view of life, death, and spirituality shifted dramatically. She felt an overwhelming desire to share the insights she had gained, though at first, she hesitated, fearing skepticism and disbelief. Over time, however, she realized that her story had the power to inspire hope and healing in others. She began speaking about her experience and eventually wrote a book, *Embraced by the Light* , which became a global phenomenon.

Betty's story resonated with millions because it spoke to universal truths: the importance of love, the interconnectedness of all life, and the reassurance that death is not the end but a transition to a greater existence. Her account encouraged readers to live with greater intention, to prioritize relationships and compassion, and to see challenges as opportunities for growth.

For Betty, the near-death experience was not an isolated event but the beginning of a lifelong journey. It inspired her to deepen her spiritual practices, to live with greater authenticity, and to help others find meaning and purpose in their lives. She often emphasized that the insights she received were not just for her but for everyone—a reminder that we are all connected, that we are all loved, and that we all have a vital role to play in the unfolding story of creation.

Today, Betty Eadie's story remains one of the most well-known and influential accounts of a near-death experience. It has inspired countless readers to reflect on their own lives and to consider the possibility that there is more to existence than meets the eye. For those who have faced loss, fear, or uncertainty, her story offers comfort and hope—a reminder that love is the essence of life and that our journey continues long after our time on Earth has ended.

Nancy Rynes: Messages from the Divine

Nancy Rynes was not the kind of person one might expect to have a profound spiritual awakening. A self-described skeptic and a scientist at heart, she had spent much of her life valuing logic, reason, and the tangible over what she considered to be unfounded beliefs in the divine or spiritual. Yet, an unexpected event changed her life forever, pushing her to the brink of death and into a realm of light, love, and wisdom that profoundly altered her understanding of existence.

The turning point came on an ordinary day when Nancy decided to take her bicycle out for a ride. Cycling was her escape —a time to clear her mind and reconnect with herself. The ride started like any other, with crisp air rushing past her as she pedaled along a familiar path. But then, out of nowhere, a truck barreled toward her. The driver, distracted, failed to see her in time. The impact was catastrophic. Nancy was thrown from her bike, her body crushed under the weight of the truck, and she was left in critical condition.

In the chaos that followed, Nancy's consciousness began to shift. She described feeling her awareness separate from her broken body. The pain, confusion, and terror of the accident dissipated as she found herself floating above the scene, observing the commotion with a strange sense of detachment. Paramedics worked frantically to stabilize her, their movements hurried but purposeful. She could see her own body—battered, motionless, and vulnerable—but she felt no fear or panic, only curiosity about what was happening.

As she hovered in this state, a sudden force seemed to pull her away from the scene of the accident. Nancy felt herself being drawn into a realm of extraordinary light. The light was unlike anything she had ever experienced—not just bright, but alive, warm, and imbued with an indescribable sense of love and peace. It was as though the very essence of this light was speaking to her, not in words, but in feelings and profound understanding. In this moment, Nancy realized she was no longer tethered to the physical world.

The realm she entered was breathtakingly beautiful. She described it as a landscape of unimaginable vibrancy and harmony, with colors and sounds that seemed to sing with life. The air was filled with an almost tangible sense of love and unity. It was here that Nancy encountered a being of light—a radiant presence that emanated wisdom and compassion. Though the being didn't identify itself in traditional terms, Nancy felt it was a guide or a messenger from the divine.

The guide began to communicate with her, sharing insights about life, love, and the interconnectedness of all things. Nancy felt herself being enveloped in a deep understanding of universal truths, as though she were being reminded of knowledge she had always known but forgotten. The guide emphasized the importance of love—love for oneself, for others, and for the world. It revealed how love was not merely an emotion but the fundamental fabric of existence, the energy that binds all of creation together.

Nancy also received messages about living with intention and purpose. The guide showed her a kind of "life review," but it wasn't focused on judgment or punishment. Instead, it was a gentle exploration of how her actions, thoughts, and choices had created ripples in the lives of others. She was able to see both the positive and negative impacts of her life, not through shame or guilt, but through the lens of growth and learning. The guide encouraged her to take these lessons and use them to live more mindfully if she chose to return to the physical world.

At one point, Nancy was shown a vision of the Earth from a cosmic perspective. She saw the planet as a living, breathing entity, interconnected with every being that inhabited it. She understood that humanity's actions affected not only the Earth but the entire web of existence. The guide encouraged her to recognize her role as a steward of the planet, emphasizing the importance of compassion, environmental care, and the collective responsibility of humanity.

As her journey continued, Nancy was given glimpses of the divine plan—a vast, intricate network of possibilities and connections that demonstrated the immense potential of human creativity and love. She saw how even the smallest acts of kindness could create profound change, rippling outward to touch countless lives in ways she could never have imagined. This understanding filled her with awe and a renewed sense of purpose.

Despite the overwhelming beauty and peace of this realm, Nancy knew her time there was limited. The guide gently conveyed that she still had work to do in the physical world, and it was her choice whether to stay in the light or return to her body. Nancy felt torn; the realm of light was so perfect, so complete, that the thought of leaving it seemed almost unbearable. But the guide reassured her that she carried this love and wisdom within her, no matter where she was.

Nancy chose to return, and with that decision, she felt herself being drawn back into her broken body. The transition was abrupt and jarring, as the pain and weight of her injuries crashed back into her awareness. She awoke in a hospital bed, surrounded by the hum of machines and the concerned faces of medical staff. Though her body was shattered, her spirit felt profoundly renewed.

The recovery process was long and grueling. Nancy had to endure multiple surgeries, physical therapy, and the emotional toll of grappling with the trauma of the accident. But she also carried with her the transformative insights from her journey. Slowly, she began to rebuild her life, integrating the lessons she had learned in the realm of light. She shifted her focus from skepticism and doubt to love, mindfulness, and intentional living.

Nancy eventually shared her story, realizing that her experience had the power to inspire and uplift others. She spoke about the importance of living with love and purpose, encouraging people to embrace their connections to one another and to the Earth. Her story resonated deeply with audiences, bridging the gap between spirituality and science in a way that appealed to both skeptics and believers.

For Nancy, her near-death experience was not just a brush with the divine but a profound awakening to the beauty and interconnectedness of life. It taught her that every moment, every action, and every choice matters, shaping not only individual lives but the collective future of humanity. Though her journey began with tragedy, it became a source of hope and inspiration—a reminder that even in the face of pain and loss, there is always light to guide the way.

Colleen Smith: A Leap of Faith

C olleen Smith's life had always been full of love, family, and laughter. She was a devoted mother and wife, known for her kind heart and infectious smile. But in the spring of 1998, during the birth of her third child, her life changed in ways she could never have imagined. What began as a joyous occasion turned into a life-threatening ordeal—one that would leave her forever transformed.

The complications started shortly after her labor began. Colleen's pregnancy had been smooth, and there were no warning signs of trouble. But as the delivery progressed, her condition rapidly deteriorated. She began to lose blood at an alarming rate, and her doctors rushed to stabilize her. Despite their efforts, her body began to shut down, and Colleen felt herself slipping away. It was then that the world around her began to fade, replaced by a strange and unfamiliar sensation.

At first, she was confused. She felt as though she was floating, weightless and free from pain. Looking down, she saw her own body lying motionless on the hospital bed, surrounded by frantic doctors and nurses. The scene should have been terrifying, but instead, she felt a profound sense of peace. She was calm, detached from the chaos below, and filled with a warmth she couldn't explain.

As she hovered above her body, Colleen became aware of a pull—a gentle yet irresistible force drawing her away from the hospital room. She found herself moving through a tunnel, the walls of which seemed to shimmer with a soft, golden light. The air was thick with a feeling of love and serenity, and Colleen felt as though she were being embraced by an unseen presence.

At the end of the tunnel, she emerged into a landscape of extraordinary beauty. It was unlike anything she had ever seen before, a garden filled with vibrant colors that seemed to pulse with life. The grass was greener than she had ever imagined, and the flowers glowed with hues beyond the spectrum of earthly colors. The air was filled with a subtle, harmonious music, as though the very fabric of this place resonated with joy.

In this garden, Colleen felt the presence of others—beings of light who radiated unconditional love. Though they didn't speak in words, their presence communicated a deep understanding and compassion. She recognized some of them immediately: her grandparents, who had passed away years earlier, and a childhood friend who had died tragically in a car accident. They smiled at her, their faces filled with warmth, and she felt their love wash over her like a wave.

One of the beings stepped forward, someone Colleen didn't recognize but who felt familiar nonetheless. This being radiated a sense of authority and kindness, and it was clear that they were there to guide her. The being told her, not with words but with an unspoken understanding, that she had a choice to make. She could remain in this peaceful, beautiful place, or she could return to her life on Earth. The choice was hers, but the being gently reminded her of her family—the husband who loved her deeply and the children who needed her.

At that moment, Colleen thought of her newborn child, whom she hadn't even held yet. She thought of her older children and how much they still needed their mother. Though the thought of leaving the garden was painful, the pull of her family was stronger. She knew in her heart that her time on Earth wasn't finished. There were things she still needed to do, lessons to learn, and love to give.

The beings of light surrounded her, offering their support and reassurance. Colleen felt their love enveloping her, giving her the strength to make the difficult decision. She turned to the guide and communicated her desire to return. The guide nodded, and the garden began to fade. Colleen felt herself moving backward, through the tunnel and toward the hospital room. The warmth and light gradually gave way to the harsh, clinical reality of her surroundings.

When Colleen opened her eyes, she was back in her body, weak and disoriented but alive. The doctors and nurses were astonished by her recovery, as they had been certain she wouldn't survive the blood loss. They called it a medical miracle, but Colleen knew it was something more. She had been given a second chance, a gift she would never take for granted.

In the days and weeks that followed, Colleen struggled to put her experience into words. How could she explain the overwhelming beauty of the garden or the unconditional love of the beings of light? How could she describe the profound sense of peace she had felt, a peace unlike anything she had ever known on Earth? She decided to share her story with her family, hoping to give them a glimpse of the extraordinary journey she had taken.

Her husband was deeply moved by her account, and her older children listened with wide-eyed wonder. As Colleen spoke, she realized that the experience had changed her in ways she hadn't fully understood. She no longer feared death, knowing that it was not an end but a transition to something far greater. She also felt a renewed sense of purpose, a desire to live her life with more intention and love.

Colleen's experience brought her closer to her family, deepening the bonds they shared. She became more patient, more forgiving, and more present in her everyday life. She began to see beauty in the small things—a child's laughter, a sunset, a kind word from a stranger. Every moment felt like a gift, and she was determined to make the most of the time she had been given.

Over the years, Colleen continued to reflect on her journey, drawing strength and inspiration from the memory of the garden and the beings of light. She felt their presence with her, guiding her and reminding her of the lessons she had learned. Whenever she faced challenges or hardships, she returned to that place in her mind, finding solace in the love and peace she had experienced.

Colleen's story is a testament to the power of love, the resilience of the human spirit, and the enduring connection between this world and the next. Her journey reminds us that even in our darkest moments, there is light to be found—a light that transcends pain, fear, and loss. It is a light that calls us to live with greater purpose, to cherish the people we love, and to embrace the beauty of life.

Though Colleen's time in the garden was brief, its impact on her life was profound. It taught her that love is the essence of existence, the thread that connects us all. And it reminded her that even in the face of death, life continues, unfolding in ways more beautiful and mysterious than we can imagine.

Thomas Welch: A Doctor's Revelation

Thomas Welch, a respected physician, had spent decades grounded in the material realities of modern medicine. He was a man of science, devoted to his patients, and firm in his belief that death marked the final chapter of existence. Near-death experiences (NDEs), in his view, were nothing more than the product of a dying brain—hallucinations, electrical misfires, or mere tricks of the mind. That belief, however, was irrevocably challenged when Thomas became the patient, facing death himself after a sudden cardiac arrest.

It was an unremarkable morning when the event that would change his life began. Thomas was at home, preparing to leave for his clinic, when he felt a strange pressure in his chest. It wasn't the searing pain he had been trained to associate with a heart attack, but a dull, foreboding heaviness that quickly spread to his left arm. He paused, brushing off the sensation as fatigue or stress—common companions in his busy profession. But moments later, as he climbed the stairs to retrieve his coat, he collapsed. The world around him dissolved into darkness.

When Thomas woke—or at least, when his consciousness became aware—he found himself floating above his own body. He could see his wife kneeling beside him, frantically dialing for an ambulance. He noted with detachment how his physical form lay crumpled at an awkward angle, as though it were merely a shell that no longer contained him. He tried to call out to his wife, to reassure her, but no sound emerged. Strangely, he felt no panic, no fear, only a profound sense of calm. A warmth enveloped him, and with it came the realization that he was somewhere else entirely.

A light appeared, unlike any light he had ever seen. It wasn't harsh or blinding but alive, pulsating with an intensity that seemed to draw him closer. He felt himself moving toward it, as though gently guided by an unseen force. The warmth intensified, wrapping around him like a loving embrace. Thomas described it later as a feeling of being utterly known—every flaw, every strength, every hidden thought laid bare—and completely accepted. There was no judgment, only love. He couldn't explain how he knew, but he felt that this light was a presence, something infinitely greater than himself yet deeply personal.

As he approached the light, Thomas became aware of other figures. They materialized out of the brilliance, their forms radiant and ethereal. He immediately recognized two of them: his parents, who had passed away years earlier. Their faces were youthful, their expressions serene. They didn't speak, but their presence communicated a message he could feel rather than hear: "You are loved. You are safe." His father, a man who had been stoic and distant in life, now exuded a tenderness Thomas had never experienced from him. His mother's smile radiated pure joy, and her presence was so vivid it brought tears to his soul.

Other figures appeared as well, though he didn't recognize them. Yet they felt familiar, as though they had been important to him in some way. He later speculated they might have been ancestors or spiritual guides. Each being exuded a sense of unconditional love and welcome, as if his arrival had been anticipated for an eternity. The light and the figures seemed to surround him, merging into an environment that felt more real than anything he had known on Earth. Colors were richer, sounds more harmonious, and every moment was infused with a profound sense of meaning.

Thomas soon found himself experiencing what he could only describe as a "life review." It wasn't like watching a movie; it was as though he was living each moment again, feeling the emotions of those he had impacted. He saw himself as a child, shy and awkward, struggling to fit in. He relived moments of triumph, like graduating medical school, and moments of regret, like a heated argument with a colleague he never reconciled. But more than the events themselves, it was the emotions of others that struck him. He could feel the pain he had caused, even unintentionally, and the joy he had brought through acts of kindness. The experience wasn't punitive—it was enlightening. It showed him the interconnectedness of all actions, how even small gestures ripple outward in ways he hadn't comprehended.

Through this review, Thomas began to understand that life wasn't about accomplishments or accolades but about relationships and love. His work as a physician, which he had often approached with clinical detachment, suddenly took on a deeper significance. Every patient he had treated was a part of this interconnected web, every moment of care or compassion adding to the fabric of human connection. He saw that the times he had rushed through consultations or dismissed a patient's concerns had deeper implications than he had realized. He also saw how his empathy, even in fleeting moments, had left lasting impressions.

The experience shifted again, and Thomas found himself standing in a landscape of indescribable beauty. It wasn't a physical place, but it felt alive—vibrating with energy, light, and music. The colors were beyond anything he had ever seen, and the air itself seemed to hum with harmony. He felt a profound sense of belonging, as though he had come home after a long journey. In this place, he sensed no concept of time or space; everything simply was. The peace and love he felt were overwhelming, filling every part of his being.

Thomas began to sense a choice. Though he felt an almost unbearable longing to remain in this realm, the light seemed to communicate that his journey wasn't finished. There was more for him to do on Earth, more lessons to learn and more people to help. He felt a wave of understanding that life was a gift, not a burden, and that returning to his physical body was an opportunity to live with greater purpose and compassion. Though the thought of leaving this place of love and beauty was difficult, he accepted the decision.

As the light and the figures faded, Thomas felt himself pulled back toward his body. The process was abrupt, and he described it as like being squeezed into a tight space. He awoke on the hospital bed, gasping for air, surrounded by doctors and nurses who had successfully resuscitated him. The warmth and brilliance of the light lingered in his memory, but he was acutely aware of the pain and frailty of his physical form. His journey, however, had left him forever changed.

In the weeks and months following his NDE, Thomas found it difficult to put his experience into words. How could he, a man of science, describe something so ineffable? But he knew he couldn't dismiss it. The love and interconnectedness he had felt were too vivid to be a hallucination. Slowly, he began to share his story, first with close friends and colleagues and later with patients. He noticed that his approach to medicine changed. No longer focused solely on diagnoses and treatments, he began to see his patients as whole beings, each with a unique journey and intrinsic value.

Thomas's skepticism about NDEs transformed into curiosity. He began researching the phenomenon, speaking with others who had similar experiences, and exploring the intersection of science and spirituality. While he couldn't prove what he had seen, he felt that his experience had given him a glimpse into a deeper reality, one where love and connection were the ultimate truths.

His life became a testament to the lessons he had learned during his journey. He worked tirelessly to infuse his practice with compassion, to repair broken relationships, and to live with gratitude for the gift of life. Thomas's near-death experience, once an event he might have dismissed in others, became the foundation of a life filled with greater purpose, empathy, and hope.

Through his remarkable journey, Thomas Welch found not just a revelation about death but a profound affirmation of life—one that continues to inspire those who hear his story.

Brian Miller: The Spirit Guides

Brian Miller was an ordinary man living an ordinary life as a truck driver in Ohio. Known for his strong work ethic and dedication to his family, he wasn't someone who spent much time pondering life's great mysteries. His days were filled with long hauls, family dinners, and the occasional weekend spent enjoying the outdoors. But one ordinary morning in 2014 turned into the most extraordinary experience of his life—an experience that would change his understanding of life, death, and what might lie beyond.

It started as any other day. Brian was at home when he suddenly felt an intense pain in his chest. The pain was unlike anything he had ever experienced—sharp, unrelenting, and terrifying. His wife called 911, and paramedics arrived swiftly, rushing him to the hospital. Upon arrival, the diagnosis was clear: Brian was having a massive heart attack. Doctors quickly realized he had a severe blockage in one of his coronary arteries—

a condition known as the "widowmaker." Time was of the essence.

Brian was rushed into surgery, but as the medical team worked to save his life, his heart stopped beating. For several minutes, Brian was clinically dead. What happened during those minutes would not only stay with Brian forever but also leave the medical staff in awe.

As his physical body lay lifeless on the operating table, Brian felt himself floating. At first, there was confusion—he was aware that something extraordinary was happening, yet he felt no fear. Instead, he was filled with a profound sense of peace. The pain in his chest was gone, replaced by a lightness that seemed to envelop his entire being. He could see the room below him: the doctors and nurses frantically working, the bright lights of the operating room, the machines beeping in protest of his failing heart. But the scene felt distant, almost unimportant, as he became drawn toward something far more compelling.

In the next moment, Brian found himself in a place unlike anything he had ever seen. He stood in a field of breathtaking beauty, surrounded by flowers of every imaginable color. The air was filled with a fragrance so sweet and pure it brought tears to his eyes. The flowers seemed to shimmer with an inner light, their hues more vibrant than anything on Earth. He could feel the warmth of the sun on his skin, yet it was not harsh—it was a comforting, golden glow that seemed to radiate love and peace.

As he walked through the field, Brian noticed that he wasn't alone. Two figures appeared before him, and his heart swelled with joy as he recognized them. They were his mother-in-law and father-in-law, both of whom had passed away years earlier. Though he hadn't seen them in years, they looked young and vibrant, free from the marks of age or illness that had taken them in life. They smiled at him, their eyes filled with an indescribable warmth.

Brian's mother-in-law reached out to him, taking his hand. He felt an overwhelming sense of love and connection, as if every unspoken word and unresolved feeling from their earthly relationship was now understood and forgiven. They didn't speak with words, but Brian understood their communication perfectly—it was as though their thoughts flowed directly into his mind. They told him how much they loved him, how proud they were of the man he was, and how they would always be watching over him.

As they walked together through the field, Brian noticed that the landscape seemed alive in a way that defied explanation. The flowers, the trees, even the air itself seemed to pulse with a kind of energy—a vibrant, loving presence that permeated everything. He felt more alive than he ever had in his earthly life, as if his senses had been heightened to their fullest potential. Every color was brighter, every sound was richer, and every sensation was infused with a profound sense of peace and joy.

But even in this paradise, Brian sensed that his time there was limited. His mother-in-law and father-in-law gently told him that it wasn't his time yet. He still had work to do, people to love, and a life to live. They assured him that they would be waiting for him when his journey on Earth was truly over, but for now, he had to return.

As they said their goodbyes, Brian felt a tug, as if an invisible force was pulling him back. The beautiful field began to fade, and the warmth of the sun was replaced by the cold, sterile light of the operating room. He opened his eyes to see the faces of the medical team around him, their expressions a mixture of relief and astonishment. Against all odds, his heart had started beating again.

Brian's recovery was nothing short of miraculous. Doctors later admitted that his survival was highly unlikely, given the severity of his condition and the time his heart had stopped. Yet, Brian felt no sense of disbelief—he knew he had been sent back for a reason.

In the weeks and months that followed, Brian struggled to find the words to describe what he had experienced. How could he explain the field of flowers, the radiant love of his in-laws, or the overwhelming peace that had filled him during those moments? He told his family about the experience, and while some were skeptical, others found comfort in his story, especially his wife, who was deeply moved by the thought of her parents watching over them.

Brian's NDE changed him in profound ways. He no longer feared death; instead, he saw it as a transition to something beautiful and eternal. He became more patient, more loving, and more appreciative of the simple joys in life. The ordinary days he had once taken for granted now felt like precious gifts, each one an opportunity to live fully and love deeply.

For Brian, the field of flowers wasn't just a vision or a dream—it was a glimpse into a reality that transcended this world. It reminded him that life is more than just the sum of our struggles and achievements; it is a journey of connection, love, and growth. And when the time finally comes to cross that threshold again, he knows he'll be greeted by familiar faces in a place of unimaginable beauty, where peace and love reign supreme.

Until that day, Brian carries the memory of his journey with him, a beacon of hope and a reminder that even in our darkest moments, there is light waiting to guide us home.

Al Sullivan: A Shared Journey Beyond

A l Sullivan's near-death experience (NDE) was unlike anything he had ever imagined. A hard-working man with little interest in spiritual matters, Al had always considered himself a practical person. He believed in the tangible and dismissed mystical ideas as fanciful notions. Yet, when his heart stopped during surgery one fateful day, he found himself drawn into an otherworldly journey that would profoundly reshape his understanding of life, death, and the mysterious connections between souls.

Al's ordeal began with what was supposed to be a routine surgical procedure. Diagnosed with a severe cardiac condition, he required an operation to repair a damaged valve in his heart. Though nervous about the procedure, Al trusted his medical team and went into the operating room with a sense of cautious optimism. As the anesthetic took hold, his awareness began to fade, and he slipped into unconsciousness—or so he thought.

What happened next defied all logic. Al suddenly found himself floating above the operating table, looking down at his own body. The scene was surreal yet crystal clear. He could see the surgeons bent over his chest, their faces tense with concentration. Nurses bustled around the room, their movements purposeful and synchronized. He even noticed the bright glare of the overhead lights and the rhythmic beeping of the machines monitoring his vital signs. Yet, none of this disturbed him. Instead, he felt a strange detachment, as though he were merely an observer, watching a play unfold.

As Al took in the scene, he became aware of a new sensation—an overwhelming sense of peace. There was no pain, no fear, only a profound calm that seemed to cradle him like a warm blanket. It was then that he noticed he was not alone. A luminous figure stood beside him, radiating an energy that felt both familiar and comforting. Though the figure did not speak, Al understood its presence as one of guidance and reassurance. He felt safe, as though nothing could harm him.

Suddenly, his attention was drawn to a presence behind him. Al turned to find a man standing there, his face illuminated by a gentle light. The man looked vaguely familiar, and as Al stared, recognition dawned—it was his deceased brother, Tommy. Tommy had passed away many years earlier, and seeing him now filled Al with an indescribable mix of joy and longing. His brother's face was youthful and vibrant, free of the sickness that had marked his final days on Earth. Tommy smiled, a smile so full of love that Al felt his heart swell.

"You're doing great, Al," Tommy said, his voice as clear as if he were standing beside him on a sunny day. "But it's not your time yet."

Before Al could respond, a shift occurred. The operating room dissolved around him, replaced by a luminous field that stretched endlessly in all directions. Colors unlike anything he had ever seen danced across the horizon, shimmering with an ethereal brilliance. Al felt as though he were standing in the very essence of life itself, a place where all things were connected. The feeling of unity was overwhelming; he could sense the presence of countless souls, each one glowing with its own unique light, yet all part of the same infinite tapestry.

In this place, time seemed irrelevant. Al felt as though he could spend an eternity here and still not grasp its full beauty. Tommy remained by his side, his presence a grounding force. Together, they walked—or perhaps floated—through this realm, and as they did, Al felt a profound sense of understanding wash over him. He saw moments from his life flash before him, not as a judgment but as a way of showing how each choice, each interaction, had rippled outward, affecting others in ways he had never realized.

Amid this exploration, Al became aware of a pull, a gentle tug that seemed to draw him back toward the operating room. He resisted at first, not wanting to leave the peace and love of this extraordinary realm. But Tommy placed a hand on his shoulder and said, "You have more to do, Al. It's not your time."

Reluctantly, Al allowed himself to be guided back. As he re-entered the operating room, he noticed something astonishing—a nurse standing near his body, her eyes wide and brimming with tears. Al could see that she was visibly shaken, her face pale as she whispered to a colleague. He didn't understand her distress until much later, but he was struck by the intensity of her emotions.

Then, with a sudden jolt, he felt himself slam back into his body. The weight of gravity returned, along with the dull ache of his physical form. Al opened his eyes to the bright glare of the operating room lights and the concerned faces of the medical team leaning over him. The surgery was a success, they told him, though they seemed hesitant to explain why they looked so shaken.

It wasn't until days later that Al learned what had happened in the operating room. As he recovered in the hospital, one of the nurses, a woman named Sarah, came to visit him. She seemed nervous, almost hesitant, as she sat by his bedside. Finally, she spoke. "Mr. Sullivan, I need to tell you something... unusual."

Al listened intently as Sarah explained that during the surgery, she had experienced what could only be described as a vision. She claimed that, for a brief moment, she had seen Al standing beside his body, accompanied by another man. Sarah described the man in vivid detail—his appearance, his warm smile, and the way he placed a reassuring hand on Al's shoulder. Al felt a chill run through him as she spoke. The man she described was Tommy.

Sarah confessed that the vision had left her shaken but also filled with an unexplainable sense of peace. "It was as if he wanted me to know that you were going to be okay," she said. "I've never experienced anything like it before."

Al was stunned. He had seen Tommy during his own experience, but how could Sarah, a stranger, have seen the same thing? The shared nature of their vision defied explanation, yet it affirmed the reality of what Al had experienced. He realized that his journey wasn't just a hallucination or a dream—it was something far greater, something that touched the fabric of existence in ways science could not yet explain.

In the years that followed, Al's life was profoundly changed. He no longer feared death, for he had seen what lay beyond the veil. He carried with him the lessons of his journey—the importance of love, connection, and the knowledge that we are never truly alone. Though he had returned to his body, a part of him remained connected to the luminous field he had visited, a place where all things were one.

For Al Sullivan, the shared NDE was not just a moment of personal transformation but a powerful reminder of the mysteries that lie just beyond our understanding. It was a story he would carry with him for the rest of his days, a beacon of light in a world that often seemed dark. And whenever he thought of Tommy, he felt a quiet sense of gratitude, knowing that his brother's love and guidance were with him always.

Janet Tarantino: Three Strikes and You're In

Janet Tarantino's journey into the extraordinary began like any ordinary day. But little did she know, her life was about to take a series of unexpected and transformative turns. Janet, a hardworking, spiritual woman, experienced not one but three near-death experiences (NDEs) at different points in her life. Each episode added layers to her understanding of existence, love, and the interconnectedness of life's moments. Her story, recounted in vivid detail, is a testament to the profound insights that can emerge from the edge of life and death.

Janet's first encounter with the other side occurred in the midst of what should have been a joyous occasion. Pregnant with her second child, Janet was in labor and awaiting the arrival of her baby. However, complications arose, and she began to hemorrhage uncontrollably. As medical staff worked frantically to save her, Janet found herself slipping away from her body. What she expected to be darkness and fear was instead a realm of incredible peace and love.

She felt herself floating, surrounded by an atmosphere that was indescribably vibrant, a tapestry of light, colors, and energy that pulsated with life. Janet became acutely aware of her existence outside her physical form. The pain and urgency of her medical crisis faded into the background as she observed her surroundings with a newfound clarity. She noticed spiritual beings, beings of light, standing nearby. They emanated an unconditional love so profound it brought her to tears. These beings seemed to be waiting patiently, observing her journey.

In that space, Janet experienced a life review, an event commonly reported in near-death experiences. This was not a judgment but a vivid playback of her life, revealing the interconnectedness of every action, thought, and intention. She felt the emotions of others as though they were her own and understood the ripple effects of her choices. It was as if her life's puzzle pieces were being assembled, forming a picture of how every moment mattered. Then came a clear message: her time on Earth wasn't over. She still had lessons to learn and love to share. Janet's consciousness gently returned to her body, and she awoke in the hospital room, grateful for the second chance to live more purposefully.

Years passed, and life seemed to settle into routine normalcy for Janet. However, fate had more lessons in store for her. The second NDE struck during a car accident. Janet was driving when her vehicle collided with another in a devastating crash. The impact left her unconscious, and once again, she found herself outside her body. This time, the transition felt more sudden and jolting. Janet described a sensation of being propelled into a space of pure light and tranquility.

Here, the experience deepened. She felt an overwhelming connection to the universe—a sense that everything was intricately linked by threads of love and energy. She encountered a being she identified as her guardian, who communicated with her telepathically. This being guided her through another life review, this time focusing on the importance of forgiveness and the release of guilt. Janet saw moments from her life where she had been too hard on herself and felt an unspoken invitation to let go of those burdens.

But there was something new about this NDE—she was shown glimpses of future events. She saw her family and loved ones going through challenges and triumphs. Some of these moments seemed trivial at first, but she later realized they were pivotal in shaping her understanding of her life's purpose. As she returned to her body, Janet was left with a profound sense of gratitude. She began to see her relationships and struggles in a new light, understanding them as opportunities for growth and expressions of love.

The third and final NDE, which Janet sometimes referred to as the one that "sealed the deal," occurred during a health crisis. A severe allergic reaction caused her to lose consciousness. As before, Janet felt herself leaving her body, but this time, she was drawn directly into what she could only describe as "the essence of love." This realm was even more vivid than her previous experiences. She felt as though she had entered the core of creation itself, where everything was imbued with a profound purpose and harmony.

Here, Janet encountered a council of spiritual beings. These beings radiated wisdom and compassion, and they seemed to carry the collective knowledge of the universe. They communicated to her that life is not a series of random events but an intricate design meant to teach us love, resilience, and interconnectedness. Janet asked questions, and though the answers often came in feelings or images rather than words, she understood them with perfect clarity.

One of the most transformative revelations came when she was shown her "life blueprint." This was a visual representation of her soul's journey, highlighting the lessons she was meant to learn, the people she was meant to meet, and the ways she was meant to grow. Janet realized that even her hardships and losses served a greater purpose, helping her soul evolve and preparing her to help others.

She was also given a choice: she could stay in this beautiful realm or return to her physical life. While the peace and love she felt made staying an attractive option, Janet knew her work on Earth was unfinished. She thought of her family and the people she could inspire with the wisdom she had gained. With that thought, she made the decision to return. She felt herself being gently guided back to her body, the spiritual beings surrounding her with encouragement and reassurance.

When Janet regained consciousness, she carried with her the clarity and insights from her NDEs. Her life was forever changed. She no longer saw death as an end but as a transition, a doorway to another realm of existence filled with love and understanding. Janet also began to view her daily life with greater purpose. She realized that every moment mattered, no matter how small, and that acts of love and kindness created ripples far beyond what we can see.

Janet's experiences compelled her to share her story, not to promote any specific belief system but to inspire others to live more fully, more authentically, and with more compassion. She became a speaker and author, detailing her journey in her book, *Dying to See* . Her message was clear: life is a gift, and every challenge, every joy, and every connection has meaning.

Through her three NDEs, Janet Tarantino discovered that life is not a series of isolated events but a beautifully orchestrated symphony, where every note contributes to a greater harmony. Her story is a reminder that love is the foundation of everything, that our lives are interconnected in ways we may not always understand, and that the moments we think are insignificant often carry the most profound meaning. For Janet, these experiences weren't just near-death—they were near-life, illuminating what it truly means to live.

Jim McCartney: The Sound of Music Beyond the Veil

Jim McCartney never imagined that a heart attack would lead him to the most profound experience of his life. A dedicated musician, Jim spent decades composing melodies and harmonies that brought joy to countless people. But no symphony he had ever written could compare to the celestial music he encountered during his near-death experience—a moment that would change him forever and redefine his understanding of music, life, and the universe itself.

It began on a quiet Sunday morning. Jim, in his late fifties, was at home working on a new composition. For months, he had been struggling to write something meaningful, something that truly spoke to the depths of human emotion. The notes seemed to evade him, and he often found himself lost in frustration. On this particular day, however, his creative block was the least of his worries. A sudden, crushing pain in his chest brought him to his knees. He clutched his chest, his vision blurred, and before he could call for help, everything went black.

Jim's next conscious thought was one of confusion. He was no longer in his home but floating above it, watching paramedics work frantically on his lifeless body. His perspective felt detached, almost indifferent, yet he could see every detail with startling clarity: the beads of sweat on the paramedics' foreheads, the rhythmic compression of their hands on his chest, the flashing red and blue lights of the ambulance parked outside. He was aware of everything, yet he felt no fear. Instead, an overwhelming sense of calm washed over him, a serenity unlike anything he had ever known.

As he observed the scene below, Jim became aware of a faint sound in the distance. At first, it was barely perceptible, like a single note drifting through the air. But as he focused on it, the sound grew louder and richer, transforming into a symphony of unimaginable beauty. The music seemed to surround him, enveloping him in waves of harmony that resonated deep within his soul. It was unlike anything he had ever heard—notes and tones that defied earthly scales, rhythms that felt as though they were alive, pulsating with the essence of creation itself.

Drawn to the music, Jim felt himself being pulled away from the earthly plane. The room faded, and he found himself in a vast, luminous space filled with shimmering light. The colors were vibrant and dynamic, shifting and blending in ways that defied description. But it was the music that captivated him. It was everywhere, a living presence that seemed to emanate from the very fabric of this realm. Each note carried an emotion so pure and profound that Jim felt as though his heart might burst from the intensity.

As he moved deeper into this realm, Jim realized that the music wasn't just something he was hearing—it was something he was *experiencing*. He could feel the notes coursing through his being, harmonizing with his very essence. The music spoke to him, not in words but in feelings and images. It conveyed truths about the universe, about love, and about the interconnectedness of all things. In that moment, Jim understood that music was more than an art form; it was a fundamental force of the universe, a language that transcended time, space, and even life itself.

He was not alone in this luminous space. Figures of light began to appear around him, their presence warm and welcoming. Though they had no distinct features, Jim recognized them as kindred spirits, beings of immense love and wisdom. One of them stepped forward, radiating a gentle yet powerful energy. Without speaking, the being communicated with Jim, conveying a message that resonated deeply within him: *"You have always been connected to this music. It flows through you, as it flows through all of creation. You have a purpose, Jim—a purpose to bring this music to the world."*

Jim was flooded with memories of his life, moments that had shaped him, both joyful and painful. He saw his younger self discovering his love for music, the long nights spent practicing, the triumphs and failures, and the relationships he had nurtured and neglected along the way. The music seemed to weave through these memories, illuminating them with new meaning. Jim realized that his lifelong passion for music had always been a part of something greater, a reflection of the divine harmony he was now experiencing.

The being of light showed him glimpses of what could be—visions of people uplifted by his music, of compositions that would inspire love, healing, and unity. Jim felt humbled and overwhelmed by the enormity of this purpose, yet he also felt a profound sense of gratitude. He understood that his life, with all its struggles and imperfections, was a part of a larger symphony, a melody woven into the infinite composition of existence.

But the journey was not yet over. The music around him shifted, becoming softer and more introspective, as if preparing him for a final revelation. The being of light guided Jim to the edge of the luminous realm, where he could see a vast expanse stretching into infinity. It was a place of pure potential, a source of endless creativity and love. Jim understood that this was the origin of the music, the wellspring from which all creation flowed.

In that moment, Jim felt a deep longing to remain in this realm, to merge with the music and become one with its eternal harmony. But the being of light gently reminded him of his purpose. *"It is not yet your time. You must return and share what you have experienced. The world needs your music, Jim. It needs the love and connection that only you can bring."*

Before Jim could protest, he felt himself being pulled back. The music faded, the luminous realm dissolved, and he was thrust back into his body with a jolt. Pain and discomfort returned, along with the distant sound of voices. He opened his eyes to see the concerned faces of paramedics and doctors hovering over him. He was alive, but he was forever changed.

The weeks that followed were a period of deep reflection for Jim. The memory of the music stayed with him, as vivid and powerful as the moment he had experienced it. He began to compose again, but this time, the music flowed effortlessly. His compositions were no longer bound by the conventions of earthly music; they were infused with the essence of the divine symphony he had encountered. Audiences were moved to tears by his work, describing it as transcendent, healing, and unlike anything they had ever heard.

Jim dedicated the rest of his life to sharing the music that had been revealed to him. He gave concerts, taught aspiring musicians, and spoke openly about his near-death experience, inspiring countless people with his story. He believed that everyone, whether they realized it or not, was a part of the universal symphony—a melody that connected all of creation in love and harmony.

In the end, Jim McCartney's journey was not just about music; it was about life itself. Through his NDE, he discovered that the universe is a vast and beautiful composition, and each of us is an essential note in its melody. His story serves as a reminder that even in our darkest moments, there is a greater harmony at work, one that guides us, uplifts us, and reminds us of the infinite beauty that lies beyond the veil.

Dr. Rajiv Parti: A Journey Through Karma and Compassion

Dr. Rajiv Parti was a man of science, a celebrated anesthesiologist who had built a life of material success. With his high-paying career, a lavish house, and luxury cars, he seemed to have it all. Yet beneath the surface of his seemingly perfect life, Rajiv was deeply unhappy. He often dismissed anything remotely spiritual as superstition, firmly believing in the clinical world of medicine and science. But in 2010, a sudden and severe illness brought him face-to-face with a profound reality he never expected—an experience that would change him forever.

It all began when Rajiv developed chronic prostate infections that required surgery. Although the procedures seemed routine, complications arose, leading to severe infections that spread throughout his body. One night, Rajiv found himself in unbearable pain, shivering with a high fever. His condition deteriorated rapidly, and he was rushed to the hospital for emergency surgery to treat a life-threatening abscess. It was during this operation that Rajiv experienced what would later be described as a near-death experience (NDE).

As the anesthesia took hold, Rajiv suddenly found himself outside of his body. He could see the operating room below, the surgeons and nurses working frantically to save his life. From this detached vantage point, he felt no pain or fear, only a sense of curiosity and awe. He observed the scene with clinical precision, noting every detail of the medical instruments and the conversations happening around him. But this was only the beginning.

Moments later, Rajiv felt himself being pulled into a tunnel, a space filled with a radiant, golden light. The light was unlike anything he had ever seen—warm, inviting, and alive. It seemed to pulsate with an energy that filled him with an overwhelming sense of peace and love. As he moved through the tunnel, Rajiv felt a profound shift in his awareness. He was no longer the man defined by his career, wealth, and achievements. Instead, he was a being of pure consciousness, connected to something far greater than himself.

At the end of the tunnel, Rajiv encountered spiritual beings who exuded compassion and wisdom. Although they didn't speak in words, he understood them perfectly through a kind of telepathic communication. They began to show him a vivid, panoramic review of his life—not as a series of disconnected events, but as a tapestry where every thread was connected. Rajiv saw himself as a young boy, filled with innocence and curiosity, and later as a driven adult, consumed by ambition and materialism. He felt the emotions of those he had interacted with, both positively and negatively. Every harsh word he had spoken, every act of selfishness or arrogance, reverberated through the life review, allowing him to feel the impact of his actions on others.

One of the most humbling moments came when Rajiv was shown scenes from his professional life. He had always prided himself on being a skilled anesthesiologist, but now he saw how his detached demeanor and lack of empathy had affected his patients. He felt the fear and vulnerability of those who had looked to him for comfort and compassion, only to be met with cold efficiency. This realization struck him deeply, filling him with regret. For the first time, he understood the profound importance of kindness and human connection.

But the life review didn't stop at his present life. Rajiv was shown glimpses of his past lives, experiences that seemed to stretch across centuries. In one life, he was a cruel landowner who exploited the poor for personal gain. In another, he was a warrior who had caused great suffering in the name of conquest. These scenes revealed a pattern of selfishness and disregard for others, a karmic cycle that had followed him into his current life. The spiritual beings explained that his current suffering—both physical and emotional—was a result of these unresolved actions. Yet, they also conveyed a message of hope: that he had the power to change, to break the cycle of karma and embrace a life of compassion and service.

As Rajiv absorbed these lessons, he was transported to a different realm—a place he described as the "River of Life." Here, he encountered his late father, a man with whom he had shared a strained relationship. In life, their interactions had been marked by anger and misunderstanding, but in this realm, his father appeared as a being of light, radiating love and forgiveness. Rajiv felt his father's unconditional love and realized that their earthly conflicts were insignificant in the grand scheme of existence. This encounter healed a wound that Rajiv had carried for years, filling him with a deep sense of reconciliation and peace.

In the final stages of his journey, Rajiv found himself in the presence of a divine being—a figure that radiated infinite love and wisdom. This being, whom Rajiv identified as an embodiment of God, conveyed a simple yet profound truth: life is not about accumulating wealth or achieving worldly success, but about love, compassion, and the interconnectedness of all beings. Rajiv was told that his time on Earth was not yet over and that he had a mission to fulfill. He needed to return to his body and use his experience to help others heal—not just physically, but emotionally and spiritually.

Reluctantly, Rajiv felt himself being pulled back through the tunnel. The warmth and peace of the light began to fade, replaced by the cold, sterile environment of the operating room. When he opened his eyes, he was back in his body, surrounded by the medical team that had saved his life. Though weak and in pain, Rajiv knew he had been given a second chance—a chance to live a life of purpose and meaning.

In the weeks and months that followed, Rajiv underwent a profound transformation. He left his high-paying job as an anesthesiologist and abandoned his materialistic lifestyle. Instead, he dedicated himself to studying spirituality, meditation, and holistic healing. He began sharing his story with others, emphasizing the importance of forgiveness, compassion, and living in harmony with one's true self. He also founded a wellness practice focused on integrating modern medicine with spiritual principles, helping patients heal on multiple levels.

Rajiv's NDE taught him that life is a precious gift, one meant to be lived with intention and love. His journey through the tunnel of light, his encounters with spiritual beings, and the lessons he learned about karma and interconnectedness became the foundation of his new life. He no longer saw himself as just a doctor or a scientist but as a soul on a journey of growth and transformation. His story continues to inspire countless people, offering hope and guidance to those seeking meaning in their own lives.

Dr. Rajiv Parti's near-death experience was not just a brush with death—it was a wake-up call, a reminder of what truly matters. It taught him that while the material world may offer comfort and status, it is the intangible qualities of love, kindness, and compassion that leave a lasting impact. His journey serves as a testament to the power of transformation and the boundless possibilities that arise when we embrace life with an open heart and a humble spirit.

Stephanie Arnold: Premonitions, Death, and the Power of Intuition

Stephanie Arnold's journey began long before her near-death experience. As a woman known for her vibrance and tenacity, she had always approached life with a pragmatic, grounded mindset. But during her second pregnancy, something began to shift—an unshakable feeling of dread crept into her thoughts. It was not vague anxiety or fleeting doubt but a deep, visceral certainty that something catastrophic would happen when she gave birth. Stephanie knew she was going to die.

At first, she brushed off the thought. She was healthy, her pregnancy had progressed normally, and there were no medical concerns. But the feeling persisted, growing stronger with each passing day. Stephanie found herself unable to ignore it. She began sharing her fears with her husband, doctors, and anyone who would listen, explaining in detail that she was certain she would die in childbirth. Some dismissed her concerns as unfounded; others reassured her that everything would be fine. But Stephanie wasn't convinced. Her intuition was unwavering.

Months passed, and the day of delivery finally arrived. Stephanie was scheduled for a routine cesarean section, a procedure she had undergone during her first pregnancy without complications. Yet as she was wheeled into the operating room, her heart pounded with the certainty that she was about to face the unimaginable. Her mind raced, replaying the warnings she had tried to voice, the urgency she had felt, and the disbelief she had encountered. Despite her best efforts to prepare, nothing could have braced her for what happened next.

As the doctors began the procedure, everything seemed to proceed normally. But moments later, Stephanie experienced a sudden and catastrophic medical emergency—a rare and often fatal condition called an amniotic fluid embolism (AFE). Without warning, amniotic fluid entered her bloodstream, triggering a cascade of life-threatening reactions. Her heart stopped. Her body went into shock. Stephanie Arnold died on the operating table.

In the stillness of death, Stephanie felt a sense of peace unlike anything she had ever known. She described leaving her body, floating above the operating room, and observing the chaos below. She watched as doctors and nurses worked frantically to save her life, their voices blending into a cacophony of urgency. Yet from her elevated vantage point, she felt detached from the scene. There was no pain, no fear—only an overwhelming calm.

Stephanie's awareness began to shift. She found herself moving through a tunnel, bathed in a warm, radiant light. The light was unlike anything she had ever seen, a luminous presence that seemed to pulse with love and understanding. As she moved closer to it, she felt a profound sense of connection, as though the boundaries of her individuality were dissolving. She was part of something greater, something infinite. It was a place where time no longer existed, where all moments were one, and where the essence of her being was fully known and accepted.

In this ethereal realm, Stephanie encountered beings of light. Though they did not speak in words, their presence communicated a deep sense of reassurance and love. They showed her glimpses of her life, a panoramic view of the moments that had brought her to this point. Stephanie was struck by the interconnectedness of it all—the way her decisions, relationships, and experiences formed a web of meaning. She saw the threads of her life weaving into a larger tapestry, part of a design that extended far beyond her understanding.

But the beings of light were not there to welcome her into eternity. They made it clear that her time on Earth was not yet over. Stephanie was shown visions of her family, particularly her newborn child. She was told that her life still had purpose, that she was needed, and that she would return to complete her journey. Although the thought of leaving the serene beauty of the light was difficult, Stephanie understood. Her love for her family gave her the strength to let go of the realm she had entered and begin the journey back.

In an instant, Stephanie felt herself being pulled back into her body. The return was abrupt and jarring, and the pain of her physical form was overwhelming. She became aware of the chaos around her—the rapid beeping of machines, the urgent voices of medical staff, and the sensation of being revived. The medical team had performed heroic efforts to save her, employing advanced techniques and sheer determination to bring her back from the brink of death.

When Stephanie finally regained full consciousness, she was overwhelmed by a flood of emotions. Gratitude, confusion, and a profound sense of awe filled her as she tried to reconcile the surreal experience she had just undergone. The visions, the light, the beings—everything felt more real than life itself. She knew that what she had experienced was not a hallucination or a dream but a profound glimpse into a reality beyond the physical.

As Stephanie recovered, she began to process the implications of her NDE. Her survival had been nothing short of miraculous. Amniotic fluid embolisms are exceedingly rare, and the mortality rate is alarmingly high. Yet she had not only survived but had emerged with a story that would change her life forever. Determined to understand the significance of her experience, Stephanie delved into research about NDEs, intuition, and the intersection of science and spirituality.

Her journey of exploration led her to connect with doctors, scientists, and spiritual teachers. She sought answers to the questions that now consumed her: Why had she been so certain of her impending death? What role did intuition play in her experience? And what was the nature of the realm she had encountered? Through these inquiries, Stephanie began to see her NDE not as a random occurrence but as a profound message about the power of intuition and the interconnectedness of all life.

Stephanie also became a passionate advocate for raising awareness about amniotic fluid embolisms and empowering others to trust their inner voice. She shared her story widely, speaking to audiences about the importance of listening to intuition, even when it defies logic or conventional wisdom. Her experience inspired countless people to reflect on their own lives, relationships, and the mysteries of existence.

Years later, Stephanie continues to describe her NDE as a transformative gift. While the experience itself was harrowing, it brought her clarity, purpose, and a deep sense of connection to the divine. She often reflects on the love and guidance she felt in the light, a love that she believes is accessible to everyone, even in the midst of life's challenges.

Stephanie's story is not just one of survival; it is a testament to the power of intuition, the resilience of the human spirit, and the boundless potential of love. Through her journey, she reminds us that life is a precious and interconnected web, filled with moments of beauty, purpose, and grace. And perhaps most importantly, she shows us that even in our darkest moments, we are never truly alone.

Tricia Barker: Angels in the OR

Tricia Barker's life changed forever on an otherwise ordinary afternoon. A vibrant college student with dreams of becoming a writer, she had no inkling that a life-threatening accident would propel her into a profound near-death experience (NDE) that would reshape her entire understanding of existence.

The day began like any other. Tricia had been running errands when a sudden swerve caused her car to skid off the road. The crash was violent, shattering her body and leaving her in excruciating pain. Her spine was fractured, her organs were damaged, and internal bleeding was threatening her life. By the time paramedics arrived, she was fading fast. Every jolt as they carried her to the ambulance sent fresh waves of agony through her body. But it wasn't long before something shifted—her pain began to melt away, replaced by an inexplicable calm. Tricia later realized this was the moment her consciousness began to separate from her physical form.

As doctors rushed to save her life in the operating room, Tricia's awareness drifted upward. She found herself hovering above her own body, watching the medical team work frantically below. Though the scene should have been distressing, she felt no fear or panic—only curiosity. She could see every detail: the precise movements of their hands, and even the rhythm of the machines beeping around her. Yet, what struck her most was the energy in the room. She could sense the intentions and emotions of each person present, feeling their hope and determination as if they were her own.

Then, something extraordinary happened. The sterile environment of the operating room began to dissolve, replaced by a radiant, otherworldly light. Tricia described it as the most beautiful light she had ever seen—soft yet brilliant, warm yet invigorating. As the light grew brighter, she realized she was no longer alone. Two angelic beings appeared beside her, radiating unconditional love and peace. They were not like the angels of traditional depictions; instead, they were luminous, ethereal, and utterly breathtaking. Their presence was soothing, as if they had been with her all along, silently waiting for this moment.

The angels communicated with her, not through words but through a deep, telepathic connection. Their message was clear: she was deeply loved and never alone. Tricia felt a wave of reassurance wash over her as if all the struggles, pain, and doubts she had ever experienced were insignificant in the grand scheme of things. She was not judged or criticized; instead, she was enveloped in a profound sense of understanding and acceptance.

The angels guided her through a life review—a vivid replay of her most significant moments. Every action, every word, and every emotion she had experienced was laid bare, not as a form of judgment but as an opportunity for growth. Tricia saw how her kindness had rippled outward, touching lives she had never even realized she impacted. Conversely, she also felt the pain she had caused others, even unintentionally. The experience was both humbling and enlightening, showing her the profound interconnectedness of all beings.

Amid this review, the angels conveyed an essential truth: the purpose of life was not to achieve perfection but to learn, love, and grow. They emphasized the importance of forgiveness, not only toward others but also toward oneself. Tricia began to understand that the trials and challenges of life were not punishments but opportunities for spiritual evolution.

After the life review, the angels revealed to her a glimpse of a higher realm. Tricia found herself in a place of indescribable beauty and harmony, where colors seemed to sing and the air vibrated with a sense of pure joy. The music in this realm was unlike anything she had ever heard—a symphony of love and unity that resonated deep within her soul. She felt completely at home, as if she had returned to a place she had always known but somehow forgotten.

Yet, as much as she longed to stay, the angels gently informed her that her journey was not yet over. They conveyed that her life had a greater purpose, one that she had not yet fulfilled. Tricia's role, they explained, was to use her experience to help others heal and find meaning in their own lives. Though reluctant to leave this heavenly realm, Tricia felt a sense of responsibility and resolve. She knew she had to return.

Before she left, the angels gave her a parting gift: a surge of divine energy that flooded her being with peace, strength, and inspiration. They promised that this energy would remain with her, guiding her as she navigated her new path. With one final embrace of light and love, Tricia found herself being drawn back to her body.

Reentering her physical form was jarring. The pain returned instantly, sharp and unforgiving. She woke to the sound of medical equipment and the voices of surgeons. Despite the discomfort, Tricia carried within her a profound sense of peace and purpose. Her ordeal was far from over; the road to recovery would be long and arduous, requiring multiple surgeries and grueling physical therapy. Yet, through it all, she held on to the memory of the angels and the truths they had shared with her.

As she healed, Tricia's life began to transform. The dreams of becoming a writer were replaced by a calling to teach and inspire others. She became a high school teacher, a role that allowed her to connect deeply with her students and encourage them to find their own sense of purpose. Her classroom became a space of compassion and understanding, reflecting the lessons she had learned during her NDE.

Tricia also began sharing her story publicly, despite initial fears of being dismissed or misunderstood. To her surprise, people from all walks of life resonated with her experience. Her words brought comfort to those grieving, hope to those struggling, and validation to those who had experienced their own spiritual awakenings. She came to realize that her story was not just her own—it was a universal reminder of the love and light that underpins all existence.

Through her journey, Tricia Barker found not only healing but also a sense of wholeness she had never known before. The angels in the operating room had shown her a glimpse of a reality far greater than anything she could have imagined—a reality where love, compassion, and interconnectedness are the ultimate truths. Her near-death experience became a guiding light, inspiring her to live with intention, to forgive freely, and to embrace the beauty of every moment.

Today, Tricia continues to share her story, spreading the message of hope and transformation that the angels imparted to her. She reminds us that even in our darkest moments, we are never alone, and that the love we give and receive is the most enduring legacy of all. Her journey is a testament to the resilience of the human spirit and the boundless possibilities of life when viewed through the lens of love.

Jeff Olsen: Love Beyond the Veil

Jeff Olsen never imagined that a single moment could shatter his world and, at the same time, lead him to an extraordinary journey of love and transformation. It was a spring day in 1997 when a family road trip turned into an unimaginable tragedy. Jeff, his wife Tamara, and their two sons—Spencer, 7, and Griffin, 14 months—were traveling on a quiet highway. The trip was meant to be a joyful outing, but in an instant, everything changed.

Jeff lost control of the car, which veered off the road and rolled several times. In the violent crash, Tamara and Griffin were killed instantly. Jeff, though gravely injured, was conscious enough to understand the devastation. Spencer, his oldest son, survived but with injuries of his own. As paramedics arrived, Jeff's injuries became critical, and he slipped into unconsciousness. What followed was a journey beyond the physical realm that would alter his life forever.

When Jeff's body could no longer bear the trauma, he felt his consciousness separate. One moment, he was trapped in the agony of his shattered body; the next, he was in a realm of indescribable peace. He described the transition as slipping out of pain and into a warm, radiant embrace. He was no longer bound by the physical. He was floating, weightless and free, surrounded by a brilliant, golden light that seemed to pulse with love.

As he adjusted to this new state of being, Jeff became aware of two figures approaching him. His heart swelled as he recognized them: Tamara and Griffin. Tamara looked radiant, more beautiful than ever, and Griffin, just a baby when he passed, now appeared healthy and full of vitality. Jeff's joy was overwhelming. He described the reunion as being enveloped in pure, unconditional love—a love that transcended anything he had ever known on Earth.

Tamara spoke to him, not with words but with a deep, telepathic connection. She reassured him that she and Griffin were safe, at peace, and filled with joy. There was no sadness in her presence, only love and understanding. Jeff could feel her gratitude for their life together and her immense love for their family. Griffin, too, radiated a sense of completeness and belonging, even though his life had been so brief. Jeff wanted nothing more than to stay with them in this serene and perfect place.

As he basked in this heavenly reunion, Jeff began to notice more about the realm he was in. It wasn't a tangible place with boundaries or structures; it was more like a state of being. The light that surrounded him seemed to emanate from everywhere, filling him with knowledge and insight. He described feeling connected to the entire universe, as if he were part of an eternal, infinite flow of love and creation.

But even as Jeff felt at home in this realm, he sensed there was a choice to be made. Tamara communicated to him that it wasn't his time to stay. His journey on Earth wasn't over, and Spencer, their surviving son, needed him. Jeff resisted at first. How could he leave this place of pure love, this reunion with the wife and child he had lost? How could he return to a world filled with pain, grief, and the crushing weight of his injuries?

Tamara's love gave him the strength to face the decision. She assured him that she and Griffin would always be with him, watching over him, and that his purpose on Earth was not yet complete. With a heavy heart, but also a newfound sense of peace, Jeff accepted his choice. He felt himself being pulled away from the light, back into the confines of his broken body.

The return was jarring. Jeff awoke in a hospital room, his body wracked with pain. His injuries were severe: shattered bones, a collapsed lung, and numerous other complications. He had undergone multiple surgeries, including the amputation of his left leg above the knee. But the physical pain paled in comparison to the emotional agony of losing Tamara and Griffin. He felt a crushing guilt for surviving the accident and struggled to find the strength to move forward.

Yet, something had changed in Jeff. The love and peace he had experienced during his NDE stayed with him, like a warm glow that couldn't be extinguished. He knew Tamara and Griffin were still with him, not in the physical sense, but as a presence that guided and comforted him. He also felt a profound connection to the divine, an understanding that love was the ultimate truth and that his life, no matter how painful, had purpose.

Jeff's recovery was grueling. He had to learn how to walk again with a prosthetic leg, and the emotional healing took even longer. But through it all, he found solace in the lessons he had learned during his NDE. He began to see life through a new lens, one that emphasized love, forgiveness, and gratitude. He poured his energy into being the best father he could be for Spencer, knowing that his son needed him more than ever.

Jeff also felt compelled to share his story. He began speaking publicly about his NDE, not as a way to relive the tragedy, but to inspire others. He wanted people to understand that love doesn't end with death, that our connections to those we've lost remain eternal. His message resonated deeply with audiences, many of whom found comfort in his words.

Over time, Jeff found new avenues for healing. He remarried and built a blended family, honoring Tamara and Griffin while embracing the new love in his life. He continued to write and speak about his experiences, sharing the profound truths he had learned during his journey beyond the veil.

One of the most important lessons Jeff took from his NDE was the realization that life, no matter how difficult, is a precious gift. He came to see challenges as opportunities for growth and found purpose in helping others navigate their own pain and loss. The love he had experienced in the divine realm became a guiding force in his life, inspiring him to live with compassion, courage, and an open heart.

Jeff Olsen's near-death experience is a testament to the enduring power of love, the resilience of the human spirit, and the eternal bonds that connect us to those we hold dear. His journey reminds us that even in our darkest moments, there is light to be found, a love that transcends time and space, and a purpose waiting to be fulfilled. For Jeff, the tragedy of loss became a doorway to profound understanding, a journey that continues to inspire and uplift all who hear his story.

Ellyn Dye: A Kaleidoscope of Creation

Ellyn Dye didn't expect her daily drive to take a life-altering turn. It was an ordinary morning, and she was en route to work, her mind preoccupied with the mundane details of her schedule. But fate had other plans. In an instant, a devastating car accident shattered the rhythm of her day—and her life. The collision left her hovering between life and death, and as her physical body lay broken, her consciousness embarked on a journey that defied everything she had ever known.

The first thing Ellyn noticed was a strange stillness. The chaos of the accident faded away, replaced by an all-encompassing calm. She found herself floating above the scene, observing the crumpled remains of her car and the frantic efforts of paramedics. As she watched, a radiant light began to envelop her. It wasn't just a visual phenomenon; it was alive, pulsating with warmth, love, and an invitation she couldn't resist.

As the light grew brighter, it pulled her into what she later described as a kaleidoscope of creation. Colors she had never seen before swirled around her, vibrant and dynamic, shifting in patterns that seemed to echo the rhythms of her own thoughts and emotions. The colors weren't just beautiful; they were sentient, responding to her presence as if engaging in a cosmic dance. Time and space dissolved, and Ellyn felt herself merge with the infinite. She was no longer just herself—she was part of something vast and eternal, an interconnected web of life and energy that encompassed the entire universe.

Within this kaleidoscope, Ellyn encountered beings of light. They radiated an overwhelming sense of love and wisdom, their forms shifting and shimmering in harmony with the vibrant colors around them. These beings were not strangers. She felt as though she had known them forever, as if they were part of a family she had forgotten until now. Without speaking, they communicated with her, their messages resonating directly in her consciousness. It was a language of feeling, of knowing, beyond words and logic.

The beings guided Ellyn deeper into the experience, showing her what she could only describe as the "fabric of creation." She saw how every thought, action, and emotion rippled outward, like a pebble dropped into a pond, touching everything else in its path. It became clear to her that life on Earth was far more interconnected than she had ever imagined. Each person, each creature, each particle of matter was part of a grand, unified whole. This realization filled her with awe. The boundaries that had once defined her world—between self and other, between life and death—disappeared, replaced by a profound sense of unity.

As Ellyn explored this realm, the beings shared with her insights about humanity's purpose. They explained that life was a creative endeavor, a chance for souls to learn, grow, and contribute to the ever-evolving tapestry of existence. Free will, they emphasized, was a powerful gift—both a responsibility and a privilege. The choices people made, the love they gave, and the energy they put into the world all shaped the collective reality of life.

She was also shown the universe in a way she had never imagined. It wasn't a cold, mechanical expanse of stars and planets; it was alive, brimming with creative energy. Every star, every atom, every heartbeat was part of a symphony of creation. Ellyn saw how this energy responded to intention and love, how it flourished when nurtured and diminished when neglected. This revelation brought her a new understanding of life's purpose: to live with love, to create with intention, and to honor the interconnectedness of all things.

During her journey, Ellyn experienced a profound sense of belonging. She felt deeply loved and valued, not for anything she had done or achieved, but simply for being. This unconditional love dissolved every fear, doubt, and insecurity she had ever carried. She understood that this love wasn't unique to her—it was the essence of existence, available to all. Every soul, she realized, was a spark of this divine energy, inherently worthy and infinitely connected.

The beings also showed her glimpses of her own life. She saw how her choices had shaped her path and how her relationships had been opportunities for growth and connection. Even the moments of pain and struggle took on new meaning, revealing themselves as essential parts of her journey. Through these experiences, she learned that life wasn't about perfection; it was about progress, about learning and evolving through each moment, no matter how difficult.

Ellyn wanted to stay in this realm forever. The love, the colors, the music—all of it felt like home. But the beings gently told her it wasn't her time. They explained that she had more to do on Earth, that her purpose was not yet complete. She protested, but their love and wisdom reassured her. They showed her how she could bring the lessons of this experience back with her, how she could live more fully and help others understand the beauty and interconnectedness of life.

With that, the kaleidoscope began to fade. The vibrant colors softened, the beings of light receded, and Ellyn felt herself being drawn back to her physical body. The transition was jarring—pain and confusion returned, and the chaos of the accident scene reasserted itself. But even as she reentered her body, she carried with her the memory of what she had experienced, a memory so vivid and transformative that it became the cornerstone of her life moving forward.

Ellyn's recovery was long and difficult, but the insights from her NDE sustained her. She began to share her story, using her experience to inspire others and to emphasize the importance of love, intention, and connection. She described the universe as a living, breathing entity, one that responded to human thought and emotion. Through her talks and writing, she encouraged people to see themselves as creators of their own reality, capable of shaping the world through their choices and actions.

Her experience also deepened her appreciation for the beauty of life. Colors seemed brighter, music more profound, relationships more meaningful. She found herself living with greater intention, savoring each moment as a precious gift. Her NDE had shown her that life wasn't about material success or external validation—it was about the connections we make, the love we share, and the creativity we bring to the world.

In the years that followed, Ellyn became a beacon of hope and inspiration for many. Her story reminded people that life was part of something much larger, something infinitely beautiful and profound. She spoke of a universe that was alive with energy and love, a universe in which every person played an essential role. Through her journey, Ellyn discovered that the kaleidoscope of creation wasn't just a vision—it was a reality, one that we all have the power to shape and nurture.

And so, Ellyn Dye's journey into the kaleidoscope of creation remains a testament to the profound truths that lie beyond the veil. It is a story of love, interconnectedness, and the boundless potential of the human spirit—a story that invites us all to see the beauty in our own lives and to live with greater purpose, compassion, and creativity.

Conclusion

The stories you've just read offer a kaleidoscope of perspectives on one of humanity's greatest mysteries: what happens when we die. From the peaceful embrace of radiant light to journeys through cosmic realms and life-altering revelations, each near-death experience (NDE) unveils a profound and deeply personal glimpse into the unknown. Yet, amid their unique details, these accounts share striking commonalities that challenge our understanding of existence and beckon us to look at life—and death—with new eyes.

What emerges from these stories is not just a narrative of what lies beyond, but a powerful reminder of what it means to be alive. Overwhelmingly, those who return from the edge of death describe a profound interconnectedness—a sense that every thought, action, and moment ripples outward, touching countless lives. They speak of unconditional love as the cornerstone of existence, a love that transcends religion, culture, and even time itself. It is a love that reminds us of our shared humanity and our place within a vast, beautiful, and purposeful universe.

As you close this book, take a moment to reflect on the insights these experiences offer. They urge us to live more consciously, to prioritize connection over division, and to see challenges as opportunities for growth. They remind us that our lives are not insignificant but are woven into a grand tapestry where every thread matters. Whether through acts of kindness, creative expression, or simply savoring the present moment, each of us has the power to shape our reality and contribute to the greater whole.

These stories also ask us to reexamine our relationship with death. Far from an end, it is portrayed as a transition—a threshold leading to a continuation of consciousness in forms we may not yet fully understand. This perspective does not diminish the pain of loss, but it offers hope and comfort, a sense that those we love are never truly gone, and that life, in all its complexity, is part of an eternal journey.

Ultimately, this collection of near-death experiences invites us to embrace life with more wonder, courage, and intention. Whether you interpret these accounts as spiritual truths, neurological phenomena, or something else entirely, their power lies in the questions they inspire and the possibilities they reveal. They remind us to focus on what truly matters: love, connection, growth, and the pursuit of meaning.

May these stories stay with you, not as a conclusion, but as a beginning—a spark that kindles your curiosity, deepens your empathy, and inspires you to live a life filled with purpose and presence. For as these extraordinary journeys have shown, the mysteries of life and death are not meant to be feared, but explored, celebrated, and embraced as part of the incredible adventure of being human.

Dear Reader,

If you have enjoyed reading this book I would be grateful if you could leave a quick review or rating. It really helps authors out when you do this, and we really appreciate you taking the time.

love and light,

Molly

Printed in Great Britain
by Amazon